ADVANCE PRAISE FOR

Epic Grace is a highly readable, intensely practical description of God's grace *in action*. It will expand (and make more readily applicable to your life) the strength, comfort, uplift, and enablement that God's grace-beyond-measure can provide the earnest seeker. Kurt Bubna's near-lyrical storytelling focuses on grace as he's discovered its power to help overcome life's blockades—a grace by which we can live beyond our limitations and experience a deeper fulfillment in life and a healthy alignment with the Father-heart of our loving God.

JACK W. HAYFORD
Chancellor, The King's University, Los Angeles and Dallas

Epic Grace describes the life experiences of pastor and author Kurt Bubna. In this well-written account, he animates his experiences and reveals God's elegant interventions. I was captivated by his life stories and left immersed in the splendor of God's amazing grace.

WAYNE CORDEIRO
Author and pastor, New Hope Christian Fellowship, Honolulu, HI

A cascade of words rushes to my mind when I think of this book: *funny, observant, insightful, genuine*. I found myself smiling a lot while reading it; it was a knowing smile, for Kurt's story is my story and your story too; it is a story of how God's strength is made perfect in our weakness.

JERRY SITTSER
Professor of theology, Whitworth University; author of *A Grace Disguised* and *A Grace Revealed*

I love the way Kurt Bubna loves his readers, shepherding them through the grace of God in difficult, pressing times. He has effectively translated his own trials so he can come alongside all of us in our quest for God's outrageous grace. Full of stories, depth, and affection, Bubna leads us to a life of possibilities.

MARY DeMUTH
Author of *The Wall around Your Heart*

Grace—the positive, loving, and forgiving action of God—is talked about in the Bible only because human beings experienced its stunning effect on their lives and wrote about it. *Epic Grace* guides us to this living water and shows us how to drink deeply. All of us who occasionally mess up in life can learn from it.

TODD HUNTER
Anglican bishop; author of *Our Favorite Sins*

Epic Grace is genuine Christianity. In this gift of the soul, Kurt Bubna invites guilt-ridden prodigals and guilt-tripper Pharisees to experience the crazy grace of God in Jesus. Such grace consumes the idiotic moves we've all made and puts us back on course to live life to the fullest before God. I encourage my fellow prodigals and Pharisees alike to read this book and journey home.

PAUL LOUIS METZGER, PH.D.
Professor of Christian theology and theology of culture, Multnomah Biblical Seminary; author of *The Gospel of John: When Love Comes to Town*

Kurt Bubna dives off the pedestal of sainthood we tend to put Christian leaders on and bares all. With an edgy wit and achingly raw, personal transparency rarely found in "pulpit people," Kurt bravely chronicles how epic grace has transformed his life, his marriage, and his relationships, throwing a life jacket of hope to fellow recovering idiots like me.

RONNA SNYDER
Author of *Hot Flashes from Heaven*

I love this book! *Epic Grace* is funny, honest, gritty, and *helpful*. Kurt reminds us that God's grace overcomes our weakness and stupidity, and makes something beautiful of our lives. His stories and the lessons he learned are grace gems; they will leave you laughing and loving God . . . and better for having read them.

JOE WITTWER
Lead pastor, Life Center, Spokane, WA

Epic Grace is the story of a life well lived . . . imperfectly receiving God's perfect grace. Kurt's disarming transparency is an inspiration to confess and own our shortcomings and live in the realm of God's unmerited favor. I am so glad to have gotten hold of this book and am so grateful that God's grace got hold of me.

MIKE MEEKS
Pastor, EastLake Church, Chula Vista, CA

Kurt Bubna is an inspired pastor who writes the way he leads and lives: with authenticity, transparency, and grace. *Epic Grace* is epic because it is the story of us all. It is the story of how God's grace can transform any weakness into strength. Read it, and you will receive it—God's epic grace.

KIP JACOB
Pastor, SouthLake Church, Portland, OR

I'm drawn to *Epic Grace* because of its no-frills approach to real-life issues of faith, struggle, and perseverance. Kurt Bubna peels back the layers of his own humanity, and his heart is exposed in the process. *Epic Grace* is a book for everyday people like you and me, craving to know more about God. I loved it.

LISA WHITTLE
Author of *Whole*; Compassion International advocate

I laughed, cried, and fist-pumped my way through this wonderful book. Be careful, though. *Epic Grace* is the kind of book that will force you into the light. Kurt's self-effacing honesty is contagious and inspiring.

JEFF KENNEDY
Pastor of discipleship, Eastpoint Church, Spokane, WA

Refreshing, honest, and uplifting. Thank God this self-proclaimed "recovering idiot" walked the path God intended him to walk. This world can use another grace warrior!

STEPHANIE VIGIL
News anchor, Spokane, WA

Kurt has done a masterful job of expounding on grace and exemplifying it through real stories—starting with his own. After reading *Epic Grace*, not only do I feel the need to magnify and share the grace of God more than ever, I also feel more empowered to share my own story with the confidence that real, epic grace is life-changing for those who receive it.

BRANDON COX
Planting pastor, Grace Hills Church, Bentonville, AR; editor of pastors.com

Let me give it to you straight, like Kurt does. I like this book. Why? Because in reading it, I find perspective, comfort, and the grace to go on. *Epic Grace* is a good book to help you keep growing, because Kurt is obviously a man who has chosen to keep growing.

MARTY BERGLUND
Senior pastor, Fellowship Alliance Chapel, Medford, NJ; author of *Choices of the Chosen*

In a world that fancies mixed images of God, Kurt Bubna describes a heavenly Father of heroic goodness. Despite his own failures, Kurt encounters demonstrations of grace so grand that God pays him in returns of startling kindness. His stories stage a drama of warmly inviting reasons for acquainting ourselves with the splendor of God's grace.

NIKI ANDERSON
Speaker, and author of four award-winning books

Kurt Bubna offers an incredibly honest, humble, and practical look at God's love and what God will graciously do as we learn to entrust ourselves fully to his faithful care, provision, and direction. There was so much with which I could personally relate. Most of all, I felt profound encouragement and gratitude for Christ's unqualified love for us and Kurt's compassionate way of pointing us to the only one who can guide us into life as it was always meant to be.

DR. JIM CORDELL
Counselor, Spokane, WA

Epic Grace is for anyone who struggles with knowing God's love. It is for the person who has warmed the pews for years, as well as for those who may not yet know who God really is. Kurt Bubna looks at life with refreshing authenticity—mistakes and all—and we see how the grace that follows after us is so complete . . . so perfect . . . so epic.

DAYNA BICKHAM
Author of *The Purpose of Chosen*

Kurt Bubna shares from the deep places of his life, his spiritual journey, his marriage, and his weaknesses. It's in these broken places that God's grace and love shine through. I felt as if I had a companion on my own difficult path, and that gave me hope. *Epic Grace* is a vulnerable, yet powerful, invitation to the table of transforming grace. We need this book.

> **MARC ALAN SCHELSKE**
> Pastor, Bridge City Community Church, Milwaukie, OR; author of *Discovering Your Authentic Core Values*

Kurt has a way of unpacking God's grace simply and honestly, revealing it in the most accessible way possible . . . through the power of his story. *Unassuming. Raw. Real.* A must-read reminder of God's heart of immeasurable grace for each of us.

> **AMY AND PAUL MILLER**
> Creative arts director and worship pastor, Life Center, Spokane, WA

I think my friendship with Kurt continues to grow because we are both just a couple of recovering idiots who are consistently overwhelmed by the epic grace of God. Everyone has a story, but not everyone recognizes God in their story. Kurt does. That's why I believe his book will help you to develop a greater awareness of God's presence in your own life.

> **WILL McCAIN**
> Lead pastor, ONE*, Spokane, WA

Kurt Bubna has given readers a remarkably candid view of his life and the subject of grace. I found myself laughing until tears rolled down my cheeks; and before I could turn the page, those tears became tears of sorrow as I felt the deep pain the Bubnas experienced. This is one of those books I will refer to again and again to provide comfort to followers of Jesus as they search for answers to life's hardest questions.

> **JEFF LAWSON**
> Pastor, Battle Lake (MN) Alliance Church

If we are sinners and God is holy, then his grace is always epic, grandiose. Kurt Bubna opens wide both his diary and the gospel to reveal how grace prevails. If you have underestimated the power of either sin or grace, this work will be a tonic to your soul.

TIM BUBNA
International worker, Christian and Missionary Alliance

In reading *Epic Grace*, I felt almost as if I were being taken by the hand through the landscape of grace. I am thankful for Kurt Bubna's transparency. Many times there can be an intentional boundary drawn between clergy and congregation. It was refreshing and inspirational to hear Kurt's honest stories interwoven in a message of God's grace.

SARAH REINHART
Ministry director, Eastpoint Church, Spokane Valley, WA

EPIC GRACE

EPIC

CHRONICLES OF A RECOVERING IDIOT

GRACE

KURT W. BUBNA

TYNDALE™
MOMENTUM

An Imprint of Tyndale House Publishers, Inc.

Visit Tyndale online at www.tyndale.com.

Visit Tyndale Momentum online at www.tyndalemomentum.com.

TYNDALE is a registered trademark of Tyndale House Publishers, Inc. *Tyndale Momentum* and the Tyndale Momentum logo are trademarks of Tyndale House Publishers, Inc. Tyndale Momentum is an imprint of Tyndale House Publishers, Inc.

Library of Congress Cataloging-in-Publication Data

Bubna, Kurt W.
  Epic grace : chronicles of a recovering idiot / Kurt W. Bubna.
    pages cm
  Includes bibliographical references.
  ISBN 978-1-4143-8504-4 (sc)
  1. Bubna, Kurt W.   2. Clergy—Washington—Spokane—Biography.   3. Grace (Theology)—Anecdotes.   I. Title.
  BR1725.B725A3 2013
  277.3'083092—dc23
  [B]   2013014467

Printed in the United States of America

19	18	17	16	15	14	13
7	6	5	4	3	2	1

For Laura, my best friend and wife of more than thirty-eight years.

Next to my love for Jesus,

I have no greater love in this life than you!

You have amazingly and patiently lived the journey with me.

I cannot imagine my life without you.

I could not ask for a greater gift from the Father than you.

And for my grandchildren . . .

Thinking about you, my four living grandchildren,

as well as my future grandchildren,

and desperately wanting each of you to know

and love God with all of your heart

was the initial inspiration for me to write this book.

I also hope and pray that when you read this, years from now,

you will gain wisdom from my mistakes and experiences.

You don't have to learn everything the hard way.

CONTENTS

FOREWORD

GRACE IS A COMMON WORD TO MOST, even those who have never experienced it. Who hasn't sung the song "Amazing Grace"? As a Christ-follower and pastor, I've contemplated grace, experienced grace, and taught about grace many times. And yet I never get tired of the topic. I never roll my eyes and say, "Really, grace again?" Honestly, I can never get enough of this core truth: Without God's grace, we *have* nothing and we *are* nothing. Grace is *everything*.

One of the things that makes grace so amazing is how multifaceted it is. It is the unmerited favor of God granting us his love and forgiveness. It is the unearned blessing of God that goes beyond our performance, our strengths, or our abilities. It is the power of God made perfect in our weaknesses. But it is also the touch of God on our broken, desperate lives—a healing touch that gives us everlasting hope.

When people first heard about my latest book, *The Circle Maker*, there were a lot of questions.

Seriously, prayer? Is there anything new that can be said about it? Don't you think that maybe it's all been covered? What are you going to bring to the table that hasn't already been said many times before?

Like grace, prayer is fairly familiar to most. But I knew God had put something in my heart that needed to be written. I knew he had given me a perspective that changed my life and could change others as well.

The book you hold in your hand, about God's grace, is that kind of book. Yes, it covers a well-known subject, but in it you will find a fresh and insightful perspective on something we can never know too much about.

Kurt's honest, heartfelt, and sometimes hilarious experiences will encourage you to walk in a grace that is truly epic. I pray that you will open your heart and allow his hard-learned lessons about grace to both challenge and encourage you in your journey.

The longer I walk with Jesus, the more I keep coming back to the simple things: *faith*, *hope*, *love*, *mercy*, and *grace*. As you read this inspiring book, may you for the first time, or the hundredth time, embrace the grace that is yours in Christ.

Mark Batterson
APRIL 2013

FIRST OF ALL . . .

I CAN BE SUCH AN IDIOT.

Really, by the most common definition of the word, I qualify, hands down. Most of what I've learned, I've learned the hard way. And I've made huge mistakes in just about every area of life.

I'm not that smart.

I'm not that polished.

I'm not that deep, profound, poetic, or philosophical.

Sometimes I feel completely inadequate and utterly overwhelmed.

I also happen to be a pastor, and no one is more surprised by that than I am. Why God would pick a guy like me to represent him is a great mystery. I'm over fifty years old, but I pray this prayer all the time: "God, please help me grow up before I grow old."

I went back and forth on what to title this book, but I knew two words had to be included: *grace* and *idiot*. Both describe my life so well. Everything I have, everything I am, and every good part of me exists because of the unbelievable grace and goodness of God. His grace is truly epic. It's larger than life and beyond my imagination. And that is a good thing, because too often in my life I've fallen into idiocy like a meteorite falling from the heavens, fast and hard with an explosive blast of burnout at the end.

I know that using the word *idiot* may not be politically correct. At times, it's hard to keep up with what's okay and not okay in our rapidly evolving cultural lexicon. That said, I assure you no offense is intended. As you read on, you'll discover I am extremely honest about some ugly past failures in my own life. So, politically correct or not, the word *idiot* just fits. It perfectly describes me and the way I've lived all too often. On the other hand, I'm an idiot saved by the heroic, sacrificial, and epic grace of God. So, in that sense, I'm a *recovering* idiot, trusting God one day at a time.

Despite my many failings, and even with all my stumbling, God, in his mercy, has taught me much about how to discover his good purpose in my life. You see, as a grace magnet, I haven't just *gone* through struggles; I've *grown* through them as well. Most important, I've learned that God deeply loves idiots—including the one behind the face I see in the mirror each morning.

I'm no one famous. Believe me, with a name like Bubna (that's right, it's pronounced *boob*-na), you would know if I were. So why should you care to read about my life? Why should my stories be of any interest?

Good questions. *Great* questions!

Here's my best answer: If you've lived long enough for life to have knocked you upside the head a few times, I suspect you might see some of your own story in mine. Not every detail or circumstance, of course, but maybe enough to learn from what I've gone through.

Maybe you share my tendency to learn lessons the hard way.

Or my predisposition to choose my own will more often than God's.

Or maybe you've known the reality of a broken heart or a broken life that desperately needs the healing touch of God.

Someone once told me that out of great pain rises the possibility for great ministry. I believe that's true. I hope by the time you're finished reading this book you will believe it too. These "chronicles of a recovering idiot" are written for those who've made some really stupid mistakes in their lives and have wondered, *How can any good come from this? How could God ever use a person like me for anything of worth?* Read on and you will see.

My friend Wayne Cordeiro, who also happens to be a pastor, author, speaker, and college chancellor, says, "We can choose either wisdom or consequences to be our teacher." I hope you will wisely learn from the consequences I've experienced. We don't always have to learn the hard way.

Maybe as you read my simple story, God's grace will win your heart. Maybe you'll discover that he can and will use anybody along the way, even idiots like you and me. Maybe you'll find out, as I have, that God delights in re-crafting our sorrows, failures, and missteps into trophies of his epic grace.

1

THE LAST TWO MILES

I came naked from my mother's womb, and I will be naked when I leave. The LORD gave me what I had, and the LORD has taken it away. Praise the name of the LORD!

JOB 1:21, NLT

SOMETIMES LIFE IS HARD. I don't mean "having a bad hair day" hard. I mean the kind of hard that knocks you down and kicks you in the teeth without any mercy. Though I've had plenty of high points in my life, I've discovered that life's most valuable and lasting lessons are often learned in the dark valleys of defeat and despair. Believe me, I wish it were not so.

I'll be honest: *Perseverance* is *not* one of my favorite words. Nobody likes to hear, "Suck it up, Buttercup." To persevere means to carry on, regardless of hardship. It's like the ant I once saw carrying a captured Frito five times its size from under a picnic table to its nest. Perseverance means you just keep going, no matter how hard or how big the challenge.

Unfortunately, we can't talk about perseverance without coming face-to-face with *suffering*. And who likes to suffer? There are so many different types of suffering. There is emotional and psychological suffering, like being verbally abused by your spouse. There is spiritual suffering, like what you experience when you're tempted to do something really bad or when you're persecuted for your faith. And there is physical suffering, such as when you struggle with a disability or an illness. All suffering brings some kind of pain.

Before we go any further, let me address something you might already be wondering: "What do suffering and perseverance have to do with grace?"

The short answer? *Everything*.

Typically, when we hear the word *grace*, we immediately connect it to *sin*. "Amazing grace, how sweet the sound, that saved a wretch like me. . . ." And that's good, because—without question—we all need the kind of grace that covers all our sin. But we also need God's grace to sustain us in the midst of our struggles. In fact, much of the grace we experience happens in the context of suffering.

God's gentle grace comforts us when we are deeply wounded.

His larger-than-life grace covers us when we are wrestling with hardship.

His empowering grace helps us to stay the course when the going gets tough.

And God's epic grace shows us how to rise above our pain and circumstances with enduring hope and faith in him.

So what does God tell us to do in the midst of suffering? He urges us to persevere—which is only possible by his grace. Look at these rather challenging Scripture verses:

Endure hardship with us like a good soldier of
Christ Jesus. 2 TIMOTHY 2:3

2

> You need to persevere so that when you have done the
> will of God, you will receive what he has promised.
> HEBREWS 10:36

> If you suffer for doing good and you endure it, this is
> commendable before God.   1 PETER 2:20

Endure. Stick with it. Hang in there. Persevere. I'd really rather not,
thank you. I'd much rather quit. I'd rather complain like a cranky
baby with a dirty diaper. I'd rather blame somebody—*anybody*—
else. Sometimes, I would rather just take a nap or numb my pain
through excessive amounts of TV or violent movies; but God
says that enduring hardship and suffering is *commendable*.

So let me say it again: To survive and even thrive in the midst
of our suffering takes grace—often in epic proportions.

One of my favorite stories in the Bible is the account of Job.
Job had it all—a great family, a great job, and a great home.
Then one day he found himself with a great loss. In fact, he
lost everything except his complaining wife. I encourage you
to read the full story of Job in the Old Testament, but for now
let's focus on the tidal wave of suffering and loss that hit him
on one horrible, unbelievably bad day:

> One day . . . a messenger arrived at Job's home with
> this news: "Your oxen were plowing, with the donkeys
> feeding beside them, when the Sabeans raided us. They
> stole all the animals and killed all the farmhands. I am
> the only one who escaped to tell you."
> *While he was still speaking*, another messenger
> arrived with this news: "The fire of God has fallen

from heaven and burned up your sheep and all the shepherds. I am the only one who escaped to tell you."

While he was still speaking, a third messenger arrived with this news: "Three bands of Chaldean raiders have stolen your camels and killed your servants. I am the only one who escaped to tell you."

While he was still speaking, another messenger arrived with this news: "Your sons and daughters were feasting in their oldest brother's home. Suddenly, a powerful wind swept in from the wilderness and hit the house on all sides. The house collapsed, and all your children are dead. I am the only one who escaped to tell you."

Job stood up and tore his robe in grief. Then he shaved his head and fell to the ground to worship.

JOB 1:13-20, NLT (EMPHASIS ADDED)

What? He fell to the ground to *worship*? Am I the only one who's thinking that *worship* is probably the last thing I would have on my mind at a time like this? Grief . . . anguish . . . suffering, yes. But worship? This can't be right. Job was a righteous man. He was a good guy who lived a good life without any cause for this kind of trouble, but trouble came calling nonetheless. And it didn't stop there.

In the next chapter of Job's story, God allows Satan to attack Job's health with a terrible case of boils from head to foot. Then three of Job's friends show up and add insult to injury by implying that Job's problems are a result of his sin.

What absolutely amazes me about this man is that he never blamed God. Instead, he said, "I came naked from my mother's womb, and I will be naked when I leave. The LORD gave me what I had, and the LORD has taken it away. Praise the name of the LORD!" (Job 1:21, NLT). Later, he added, "Though he slay me, yet will I hope in him" (Job 13:15). In other words, even if this struggle—or God himself—kills me, I still choose to trust in him.

I don't know about you, but I think I would blame God. And yet somehow, Job kept going. He persevered. And not only did he keep moving forward, he found it in his heart to *worship*. Somewhere along the way in his lifelong journey, Job figured out that persevering through life's struggles is better than quitting—and cursing God in the process. That's grace.

A Taste of Job's Sorrow

I wish I could tell you that I have no idea how Job must have felt. I really wish I could, but I can't. I know the agony and grief that pierces the soul and plunges it into a deep and dark emotional fog. I know how heartbroken Job was over the loss of his precious children.

On Saturday, March 15, 2008, my wife and I found out that our daughter-in-law was in premature labor—just seven months along—and that an ultrasound had indicated complications with the baby. We quickly packed, jumped in the truck, and drove as fast as we could from Spokane to Portland, where our kids live. It was dark and raining most of the way. Laura and I talked very little during those five hours. We simply prayed. A lot.

About an hour outside of Portland, the cell phone rang. It was my son, Nathan. He could barely speak as he told us through his tears that his newborn son, Phineas, was gone. The little guy had survived the delivery, and he was beautiful; but due to complications beyond anyone's control, and because his lungs were underdeveloped, he lived for only about an hour.

Laura and I pulled off the highway and just wept, more deeply than we had ever wept before. I wept for my son and his dear wife. I wept for Laura and myself. I wept for Phineas. I had never known that kind of pain before. It was like a Mack truck was crushing my chest and I couldn't breathe. It was unbearable.

When we walked into the hospital room, Nathan was holding his lifeless son, and the pain in his eyes broke my heart anew. At that moment, I would have done anything to change what had happened. Without hesitation, I would have exchanged my own life for that of Phineas, if only I could have. I grabbed my son, and for one brief moment father, son, and grandson embraced.

I kept thinking, *This isn't the way it's supposed to be. This isn't right. God, how could this be happening? No grandfather should outlive his grandson.*

For a long time, I agonized over this tragic loss to our family. God and I had some very long talks through tidal waves of tears. By God's grace, our family survived, but it took a while for me to come to the place where I could fall on my face and worship.

In the weeks that followed Phineas's death, I learned that God can handle my pain and anger. He drew me very close and held me tight, even when I was furious with him and confused. The depths of his grace sustained and carried me when all I wanted to do was crawl into a deep hole and hide.

I discovered that he really is "the God of all comfort" (2 Corinthians 1:3). He knows how hard it is to lose a Son, so he knows how best to encourage us through the agony of death and loss.

During this season, I also experienced the power of true

friendship. Many dear friends stood by us during those dark days. Unlike Job's friends, who offered little more than spiritual platitudes, our friends embraced us with a love that said, *We're going to stick with you, no matter what.*

I also rediscovered the power of fixing my eyes on Jesus in the midst of great struggle. What I can never do, he has already done. What is impossible for me in my own strength and wisdom is HIMpossible through God's grace.

Years before the loss of my grandson, Nathan and a friend had joined me at mile twenty-two in my first marathon. I had hit the wall and was ready to quit. My mind and body were screaming at me to give it up and call it a day. Nathan could see the defeat in my face. He knew his dad pretty well.

What he did next will forever stand as one of the greatest father-son moments in my life. He said, "Dad, you can finish; just fix your eyes on me and we'll get through this together."

Before I could even respond—and a few choice words *did* come to mind—Nathan pulled right in front of me and paced me to the end. I don't even remember that last couple of miles, but I do remember locking my eyes on Nathan's feet and literally taking it one step at a time.

When we want to quit and everything in us is *D-O-N-E*, fixing our eyes on the "author and finisher of our faith" (Hebrews 12:2, NKJV) will get us to the finish line. We are not running alone.

Margaret, My Hero!

I have a friend named Margaret. We actually haven't been in contact for many years, but I still consider her my friend and

I will never forget her. Margaret has cerebral palsy, and she has suffered more than any other person I've ever known.

Getting out of bed in the morning is a struggle for Margaret. Getting dressed is hard. Brushing her teeth is difficult. She needs help getting into her wheelchair. She needs help in the bathroom. Getting food from the plate to her mouth is an unbelievable battle. She is extremely bright and has amazing insights into life, but talking is hard too. And at the end of the day, she needs help getting ready for bed and getting into bed—only to start the whole struggle over the next morning. Over the course of my life, I've gone through my share of struggles—both miniscule and mammoth. But I have never been through as much as Margaret goes through every day of her life. I thought the last two miles of a marathon were tough, but they are nothing compared to her struggles.

Margaret will never be famous. Her pool of friends is actually quite small. She will never win any athletic awards or trophies. Nevertheless, to me she is a hero. She is, without a doubt, one of the greatest and bravest people I've ever had the pleasure of knowing.

We were part of the same church for several years when I was younger. She always sat in the back left-hand side of the auditorium in her wheelchair.

One day I came in late, as the congregation was singing the old chorus that goes, *"I love you, Lord, and I lift my voice to worship you, O my soul, rejoice!"* and here's what I saw—it is an image burned into my soul for all eternity: Margaret was in her usual spot, but she had her crippled and shaking hands as high in the air as she could lift them. She had a stream of saliva flowing from her lips (which was a normal part of her condition) and tears pouring down her face, which bore a crooked smile. Her eyes were closed, and she was singing with all her heart.

Everything Margaret tried to do was a struggle. But she knew how to persevere, and nothing was going to get in the way of her love for God. Nothing was going to keep her from giving him everything she had.

As I stood in the back and watched her, I wept. In fact, even now, just thinking about it, tears are coming to my eyes. I was amazed by her magnificence. No model on a runway could ever compare with her beauty. No queen on earth could ever measure up to her grandeur. I was blown away by her love for God. I was humbled by her ability to press through all the physical issues as she worshiped. I was awestruck by this wheelchair-bound woman walking in the fullness of the grace of God.

After church one day, I stopped Margaret on her way out. I got down to eye level with her and said, "Margaret, how do you do it? How do you deal with what you deal with and keep on going?"

She smiled her crooked smile, looked me in the eye, and said (struggling with every word), "Every day is another day to show my Jesus how much I love him."

She didn't get bogged down in the struggle.

She didn't focus on the hardships.

She wouldn't allow herself to grovel in self-pity.

She refused to be defined by her loss.

Instead, she saw every day as another day to show *her* Jesus how much she loved him.

Now, for someone whose body more or less works the way it's supposed to, Margaret's response might seem unfathomable. But it's a perspective wrought on the anvil of a daily commitment to draw close—and stay close—to God. Margaret was well-acquainted with suffering, but more than that, she knew God's grace. She lived it, breathed it, and radiated it to everyone she encountered.

Joy, Patience, and Faith

There are many things I still don't understand. But I refuse to be one of those guys who says, "Just grin and bear it!" I've had enough times when I didn't want to grin and I really didn't want to bear it, because it hurt too much.

I struggle from time to time with the canned Christian clichés about "a greater purpose" and the sovereignty of God. I know God can bring good out of any evil, but when you're in the middle of the evil, the darkness can seem pretty overwhelming.

I know we live in a broken world with broken people, and we can't blame God for the consequences of evil or our sinful choices. I know what the Bible teaches about suffering, but my heart still aches with the all-too-often real downside of life on this planet.

Why did my grandson die?

Why didn't God answer my prayer the way I wanted it answered?

How could a good God let a good man like Job suffer so horribly?

Why was Margaret born with cerebral palsy?

Why is there so much suffering and despair in the world?

I don't know the answers to these questions. And this side of eternity, I may never know.

But here's what I do know; here's what I hold on to; here's

what keeps me going and persevering: It is the simple truth from a children's song I learned in Sunday school a long time ago: *Jesus loves me.*

Maybe that sounds like a pat answer or just another Christian cliché, but let's go a little deeper: *Who* is this Jesus who loves me—and loves you? The Bible says he's "a man of sorrows, acquainted with deepest grief. . . . Yet it was our weaknesses he carried; it was our sorrows that weighed him down. . . . He was beaten so we could be whole. He was whipped so we could be healed" (Isaiah 53:3-5, NLT). This Jesus who loves you and me knows what it means to suffer—and he carries our sorrows. That's why we want to stay right on his heels and close to him; that's where we can know and experience his epic grace in a way that is beyond our ability to fully fathom.

Some time ago, my son and daughter-in-law took my granddaughter Adelle to the doctor for her very first set of immunization shots. She cried. It hurt. Mom and Dad cried. It hurt them to see her in pain. I cried just hearing the story. Our love for Adelle is so strong, so deep, and so compassionate that her pain caused us pain.

I think that must be how it is with God. When we hurt, he hurts. When we ache, he aches. *It's what love does.*

Are you hurting right now? Does it feel like you can't go another day, another step? I know from firsthand experience that the last two miles of a marathon are the hardest. But we have to keep going. Life is brutal sometimes, but you can take your pain to the One who loves you more than his own life, and fix your eyes on him.

As you learn to persevere, stay close to God. Take to heart the apostle Paul's encouragement: "Be joyful in hope, patient in affliction, faithful in prayer" (Romans 12:12). Above all, remember this promise from the One who carries your sorrows: "I will never fail you. I will never abandon you" (Hebrews 13:5, NLT).

2

DRIVEN BY DESTINY

"For I know the plans I have for you," says the Lord.
"They are plans for good and not for evil,
to give you a future and a hope."
JEREMIAH 29:11, TLB

DESTINY. Even the sound of the word is cool. It stirs our blood and fans the flames of passion in our hearts. It can fill our minds with wonder and our imaginations with awe. With a sense of destiny, men and women throughout history have accomplished great things. Christopher Columbus, Leonardo da Vinci, Galileo, Joan of Arc, Amelia Earhart, Mahatma Gandhi, Martin Luther King Jr., Homer Simpson. Okay, maybe not Homer, but you get the idea. These incredible people changed the course of history through their visionary leadership birthed out of a deep sense of personal destiny.

Destiny matters. Discovering who we were created to be, and what we were made to do, makes all the difference in the world. I'm not saying we're all destined to be superheroes or famous celebrities. In fact, very few people will have a global impact or be remembered beyond their local sphere of influence. But we all were created for significance, and we all need to find our God-given niche—what we were made for and why we exist.

Discovering our destiny is important, because when we understand our purpose, it brings a clarity and conviction to our hearts that will help keep us on track and save us from wandering in futility. It will also lead us to the joy that comes from living in our God-designed sweet spot—that place where we can have the greatest impact.

In the fall of 1975, I enrolled at Glendale Community College. I was eighteen years old and recently married. My dream and goal was to become a fireman. Specifically, I wanted to be a paramedic, or what today we would call an EMT. If I'd thought I had the brains or the patience, I might have pursued becoming a doctor. Since I lacked both, I thought becoming a paramedic would be a good alternative. That doesn't mean paramedics aren't smart and patient, only that I really had no idea what it took to become one. I knew I liked helping people, and I really liked the idea of driving fast on my way to rescue someone. So those were my primary qualifications.

There was one little problem with my plan. The whole world—well, it *seemed* like everybody—had the same idea. One of the top television shows at the time was a program called *Emergency!* and guess what it was about? That's right—paramedics in the LA Fire Department. There wasn't a young, red-blooded American male who didn't at least think about becoming just like Roy DeSoto and Johnny Gage (the heroes of the show).

In fact, when I applied to the local training program, they were accepting only one in every hundred applicants. They put us through a rather extensive physical and psychological test, as well as a written exam. I did okay with the tests, but I knew that only the best of the best would make it.

I was told it would be six to eight weeks before I would hear whether I'd been accepted into the program. Every day, I wondered, worried, and waited. Like I said, patience was not one of my strong suits, so the wait was killing me.

It would be an exaggeration to say that I felt a sense of destiny about becoming a fireman. But somehow I knew I was made to help people. Like a lot of guys, perhaps, I see myself as a rescuer—you know, the old knight-in-shining-armor idea— and so becoming an EMT seemed to make sense, and it certainly was exciting. Deep down, however, I started to wonder about something else. Was this what God had made me for? Was this his plan for me?

Ain't No Way!

Growing up as a preacher's kid (PK) left me with one strong conviction about my future career: I would never be a pastor. I would love and serve God in some other capacity, but not in the church.

On more than one occasion I told God, "You can have my heart, my money, my loyalty, and I'll even be a deacon if you want, but professional ministry is not for me."

I think God just smiled and nodded when I made those bold declarations. He had a plan for me and he knew that sooner or later I'd figure it out.

After about two or three weeks of waiting to hear if I'd been accepted, I was asked by a friend whether I'd ever thought about going to Bible school. I almost laughed out loud.

"You've got to be kidding me," I said. "Why in the Sam Hill would I go to Bible school?" I was trying to make a point. But what he said next really got under my skin.

"I don't know. It just seems like you'd be a good preacher or something."

"*Or something*" was right. One of the things I hated most about school was all the oral book reports the teachers used to assign. I was terrified of public speaking. I loathed the idea of getting up in front of people to talk. I'd rather go to the dentist.

Me, a preacher? That ain't never gonna happen.

God just kept smiling.

Not only did I have some major baggage about ministry and no natural skill in public speaking, I also had absolutely no desire to teach. Nevertheless, my friend's question haunted me on an almost daily basis. The more I tried to run from it, the more it seemed to chase me.

A French poet by the name of Jean de La Fontaine once said, "A person often meets his destiny on the road he took to avoid it." I hate it when people are right like that. Ah, but what did he know anyhow?

One day, after checking the mail for the hundredth time looking for a reply from the paramedic program, I told my dear wife, Laura, what my friend had said. I was hoping she would laugh it off with me. I was counting on her to affirm the ridiculousness of the idea of me as a preacher. To my utter dismay, she said, "Well, the Lord told me I would be a pastor's wife someday."

My first thought was, *I wonder who she's going to marry after me?* I don't remember what I said to her, but I'm sure it wasn't very nice.

My heart was in some major turmoil. "God, why are you doing this to me?"

A few more days passed. A few more sleepless nights. Many more trips to the mailbox. Then one morning during my devotions, I read this passage in Jeremiah:

The Lord said to me, "I knew you before you were formed within your mother's womb; before you were born I sanctified you and appointed you as my spokesman to the world."

"O Lord God," I said, "I can't do that! I'm far too young! I'm only a youth!"

"Don't say that," he replied, "for you will go wherever I send you and speak whatever I tell you to. And don't be afraid of the people, for I, the Lord, will be with you and see you through."

Then he touched my mouth and said, "See, I have put my words in your mouth! Today your work begins, to warn the nations and the kingdoms of the world. In accord with my words spoken through your mouth I will tear down some and destroy them, and plant others, nurture them, and make them strong and great." JEREMIAH 1:4-10, TLB

Talk about a wake-up call. Words can hardly describe how hard this hit me. It was as if God had ripped these words out of time and history and had spoken them just to me. I was both amazed and devastated. *Here I am, just minding my own business, and now God shows up and wants to run everything.* At least that's how I saw it at first. But starting that day, something began to happen in my heart. I started to sense a divine call, a destiny from God, and it began to change me.

For a week or so, I prayed my heart out. I knew that this decision would transform my life. I knew I was at the proverbial fork in the road. I knew in my gut I was made to help people, but this was *way* beyond what I'd ever thought or dreamed.

Early one morning, I was driving to school. Thinking. Praying. Pondering. And here's what God spoke to my heart that day: "You can do *anything* you want to do and I will bless and use you, but you were made to serve me as a pastor."

I knew exactly what that meant. It meant that God knew a lot more about his plan for my life than I did. It meant he had created me and designed me for a purpose that I had rejected because of fear. I didn't hear an audible voice. The heavens didn't part, and there wasn't any handwriting on the wall. But I had a moment of revelation that changed me and redirected the course of my life.

Ch-ch-ch-changes!

I knew I could be a fireman and a paramedic and serve God, but I also knew that *good* is not always *best*. God's best for me was to be a pastor.

I'm not saying that being a pastor is better than being a fireman, or that pastors are more important than firemen. I mean, really, if you think about it, we both put out fires. So please don't think you have to become a missionary or a minister to really be in your God-ordained sweet spot. Going into full-time Christian service doesn't require working for a church. For most people, the best place to serve as a Christ-follower is as a butcher, a baker, or a candlestick maker.

Tragically, I've seen too many well-intentioned people end up in professional ministry because they thought it was the only legitimate way to serve God. Hogwash! The primary issue is not vocation, but obedience. We are all called to function in full-time Christian service to God, and this happens best as we discover our niche and serve God with all our hearts, no matter what he leads us to vocationally. This is how we experience our God-ordained destiny and his best for us—by doing whatever it is we were made to do.

"A person often meets his destiny on the road he took to avoid it." That moment in my baby-blue Dodge Duster on the road to college was a God moment for me. Everything changed—but more important, *I* changed. I let go of the reins. I surrendered. I said *yes* to God.

No matter what God has planned for you, the key to seeing it happen is in your hands. Will you let go of your plans in favor of his? Will you surrender your will to the Father? Will you say *yes* to him even when it's scary and way outside your comfort zone?

A huge part of entrusting our lives to God is believing that his grace is sufficient and will bring about his best for us. We can sing about grace until the cows come home, but to truly live in it, we must rest in it and believe that God's plan is always for our good. We must embrace his grace in *every* area of our lives—including our vocation. If God's grace means his unmerited favor, then we want to know that grace both relationally and vocationally. Epic grace is not just a theological concept; it is a practical reality we are to live in day in and day out. All the time. Everywhere.

My story gets even better. Guess what I received in the mail that very day? You guessed it—a letter congratulating me for my acceptance into the paramedic training program. What a sense of humor God has. On the same day I chose his way, he made it clear to me that I actually did have options. Being a pastor wasn't my second choice. It wasn't because I didn't have anything better to do or any other possibilities. It wasn't because I feared God's wrath or the fires of hell if I decided to become a fireman. God would have blessed me and used me either way—but *his* way was better. It always is.

The following June, we moved to Eugene, Oregon, to attend Bible school, and I have never looked back and questioned whether that was God's plan or not. Even when I later fell away and left the ministry for a season (more on that in the next chapter), I still knew what I was called to do.

The Process of Discovery

About now, you might be screaming, "Fine! I need to discover my God-given destiny! But I don't know how to get there from here."

There's no magic formula or five-step program, but here are some things that will help you in your journey of discovery:

- First, what do you believe God is saying? What does that still, small voice of the Holy Spirit whisper to you in moments of reflection? What does God seem to be highlighting for you from his Word?
- What are others saying? Are there voices of confirmation in your life that underscore what you think you've heard from God? Wisdom from other godly men and women

in your life is imperative. Please don't go off half-cocked with "a word from the Lord" that has not been affirmed by people who love you and love God. When I made the life-changing decision to pursue the pastorate, my wife, my friends, and my pastor all said, "Sounds like God."

- Sometimes it's helpful to ask yourself: Which option requires more faith? Which path will require more trust in God? Not always, but often, the more difficult road is the way he's chosen for us. Why? Because that is the way that keeps us humble and dependent on him. For the record, the way of grace is always good, but it's not always easy.

- Here's the last thing I'll mention: It's good to *follow the peace.* The road before you may scare you, but once the choice is made, is there a peace in your heart that goes beyond human understanding? The Holy Spirit is called the Comforter, the One who comes alongside, and with his presence comes peace. By the way, peace is not the absence of fear; it is having an almost unexplainable God-confidence in the midst of fear and uncertainty.

A British comic writer by the name of Douglas Adams put it this way: "I seldom end up where I wanted to go, but almost always end up where I need to be." With God, this is so true! He's patient. He never gives up on us. Sometimes we veer off the path. Sometimes we wander in confusion. Sometimes we vacillate between stubbornness and cluelessness. But God, in his gentle way, faithfully leads us to discover our destiny in him. Eventually, if our hearts are yielded to him, he gets us precisely where we need to be.

I've been a pastor for more than three decades now. I still get nervous speaking to my church. I'm still not entirely comfortable with standing in front of a crowd, now numbering in the thousands at our church. But I wouldn't trade one day of pastoring for anything else. It is my destiny. It is what God made me to do.

Jean Nidetch, a cofounder of Weight Watchers, once said, "It is *choice*—not *chance*—that determines your destiny."

I love the fact that God always gives us a choice.

But we must choose to love him, or not.

We must choose to embrace his epic grace, or not.

We must choose to say yes to him, or not.

We must choose to follow him or to go our own way. And without question, our choices determine how quickly we will discover and live out our God-given destiny.

I don't know what God has in mind for you. I don't know your destiny. I don't know what he made you to be or what he has for you to do. But this I do know: He knows the plan, and he always has a purpose for you. You might be thinking, *How do you know this, Bubna?* I know it because the Bible presents God from Genesis to Revelation as the ultimate planner. He never wanders from day to day wondering what might happen next. He knows. He's always working. And he has a plan for your life that he prepared for you long ago. In fact, according to the apostle Paul, "we are God's handiwork, created in Christ Jesus to do good works, which God prepared *in advance* for us to do" (Ephesians 2:10, emphasis added).

Here's some truth you can take to the bank: God *always* has a plan for *all* of his kids; it is *always* a good plan, not an evil one; and it is *always* designed to give us hope, even if we are in

22

captivity. Even his discipline is for our good and to give us hope (Hebrews 12:5-11). The truth and reality of God's sovereign plan for his people is seen in the way he has dealt with Israel and the way he deals with the church.

Your destiny may be in the marketplace as a retailer or sales professional, serving God with all your heart. It may be in the business world or in construction. You might be called to be a teacher or a dry cleaner. Maybe it is to be a stay-at-home mom and homemaker. What is important is being who God made you to be and being where he wants you to be. What's important is finding and living your God-given purpose in this world. Nothing else matters more than following Jesus wherever he leads. That is your ultimate destiny, and that is the result of his epic, larger-than-life grace.

So what's holding you back from the great adventure of discovering your destiny?

3

PRONE TO WANDER

My brothers and sisters, if one of you should wander from the truth and someone should bring that person back, remember this: Whoever turns a sinner from the error of their way will save them from death and cover over a multitude of sins.

JAMES 5:19-20

TRAGICALLY, I HAVE BEEN MY OWN WORST ENEMY. Having a bit of attention deficit disorder, I've often struggled to stay the course. I'm often too easily distracted by my own emotions and desires. In my early twenties, I went through a season when I wandered far from God.

In June 1978, my wife and I moved from Eugene, where I was a youth pastor for a huge, robust congregation of believers, to Spokane, where our intention was to help and support our friends Joe and Laina Wittwer with a church in its infancy, a little place called Life Center.

We were excited. We loved Joe and Laina and considered it a privilege to join them in this new adventure. We knew the church would be too small at first to hire me as its youth pastor, so I'd have to get an outside job as well, but it was a sacrifice worth making. What we didn't know was how unbelievably hard our life was about to become.

Because I needed to financially support my wife and newborn daughter, a friend of a friend convinced me to get my insurance license and sell life insurance. The outfit I went to work for did two things to help me get started. First, they gave me a list of phone numbers to cold call. (Tell me, how excited do *you* get when a salesman calls you out of the blue to sell you something you either don't want or already have? I'm the same way. It was miserable. I hated it.)

The second thing my boss did was send me out to the streets to knock on doors. Oh yeah, that's better. Now, instead of an impersonal phone rejection, I would have people slamming doors in my face.

I worked hard, but I am a horrible salesman. That job lasted less than two months, and by then I was not only discouraged, I was getting financially desperate.

I had spent most of my high school years and my first year of college working in a grocery store. In fact, I was still a card-carrying journeyman in the Retail Clerks Union, so I went back to the biz I knew. I ended up working for Safeway. It was not a bad job and the pay was decent, but for me it felt like a *big* step backward, and I was miserable there, too.

I really wish I could tell you that even though my employment status was a struggle, the church was going great. Unfortunately, it wasn't. When we first arrived, the church had about fifty or sixty people attending; but within a matter of what seemed like weeks, thirty or forty of those people were gone.

Laura and I lived next door to the church building. One morning, as I walked out my door to go to the job I hated,

I heard Joe in his office wailing loudly, "Oh God, why did you bring us here?"

Just the boost of confidence I needed in the midst of my own personal misery.

"God, why *did* you bring us here?"

Joe was and is a great teacher, and I expected he would draw hundreds of people to the church in no time. I figured that within a matter of just a couple of months, he'd be offering me a full-time, paid position. I expected a great adventure and the thrill of victory. What I got was the agony of defeat.

Here's a little lesson I learned a long time ago: Unmet desires are the source of most of the conflict and many of the struggles in our lives. When we don't get what we want, or when and how we want it, life can get pretty ugly.

The Plot Thickens

In the midst of all this, my parents decided to move to Spokane. At first, I saw this as a good thing, the one bright spot in what was becoming a tragic saga. However, that bright spot quickly turned into another nightmare.

My mom and dad had never had a good or healthy marriage. Over the years, my dad, who was a pastor, had been unfaithful on multiple occasions. I knew that. I had grown up in his home. What I didn't know was how horrible things had become between my parents. You can imagine what an emotional train wreck this was for me as I was trying to move ahead with my own journey into pastoral ministry.

My dad's addiction to prescription drugs had taken its toll on his life and his marriage. I will spare you the gory details, but all of this led to an intervention in which my mom and I confronted my dad with two options: get professional help immediately or move out of the house right now.

Within a week, he was in a hospital going through detox. Tragically, though, the damage to his marriage was done. Within a few months after completing detox, my dad left home and moved far away, never to return.

During our time in Spokane, Laura was pregnant with our second child. To say that our firstborn, Jessica, had been a challenge would be an understatement. She had colic as a baby and a very strong will. Nonetheless, we loved kids and wanted more, so just eighteen months after Jessica was born, we had our son, Nathan.

He was beautiful—a gift from God. However, the day we brought him home from the hospital, the doctor told us to keep an eye on him because he was a bit jaundiced. The doc said, "If he gets any 'tanner' and doesn't seem to be improving, bring him in right away."

A couple of days later, he looked like he lived in Hawaii, not Spokane. His eyes were very yellow, and he was extremely lethargic.

When we brought him to the pediatrician's office and they took a blood test, his levels were off the chart. In fact, the doctor said they were dangerously high and he wanted us to readmit Nathan to the hospital immediately.

We were devastated. What did he mean by "dangerously high"? What were they going to have to do for him? Why was this happening on top of everything else? Nobody wants to take their baby back to the hospital.

Nathan ended up having a blood transfusion, and he spent

several days naked and blindfolded under what is called a bili light. A bili light is a phototherapy tool used to treat newborn jaundice, which is technically called hyperbilirubinemia. All of this was necessary because severe and untreated jaundice can cause brain damage leading to cerebral palsy and a long list of other horrible problems, not to mention death.

We couldn't sleep. We couldn't eat. We could not even touch or hold our precious baby boy. All we could do was hold each other and cry as we looked through the glass window that separated us from our little boy in the neonatal intensive care unit.

D.O.N.E.

Good grief! Could it get any worse? I hated my job. I was deeply disappointed in the church. My parents' marriage imploded right before my eyes, and they ended up divorced. Now it appeared my only son might end up with long-term health issues due to something completely out of our control.

I was so angry, and I became bitter. I didn't blame my parents, Joe, the doctors, or myself. I blamed God.

"You said you would take care of us, God. You said you would bless me. *You* brought me to this armpit of a town. This is *your* fault, God, and if this is the best you can do for me, I'm done with you!"

It didn't happen overnight, but my trust in God was shattered. I no longer believed he had my best interest in mind. I was done counting on him for anything, and I decided I had to take matters into my own hands.

I can be such an idiot.

We spent thirteen months in Spokane—the worst thirteen

months of my life. Finally, I told Joe we were done, that "God had released me" and we were moving back to Southern California. Why do we Christians tend to spiritualize our own stupidity? Truth is, God hadn't released me, but I had released him.

Leaving Spokane, rather than staying the course, was one of the biggest mistakes I've ever made. I left bitter, not better, and it was the beginning of the only time in my life when I walked away from God. I left the ministry and any desire to ever be a pastor again. I left any confidence I had that God had a good plan for my life. I eventually abandoned all my connections with the church, and I almost left my wife. I call that period of my life "the dark ages" because my heart was far from God and full of darkness.

For the better part of two years, I wandered off on my own. I drank hard. I partied hard. I did things too shameful to speak of. Looking back now, it's hard to believe how quickly I became such an efficient and effective idiot. In my anger and bitterness, I rationalized my sin and excused my stupidity.

When we've known the truth and life that comes from a relationship with God, why is it so easy for us to walk away from it? Why are we so prone to wander? How can we know what's right and still choose what's wrong—and not even care? It's a scary place to be, and if you've ever been there, you know exactly what I mean.

One warm and breezy fall evening in Southern California, I had just gotten home from a bar when the phone rang. It was an old friend named Steve Overman. For weeks, he had been meeting me for lunch. He knew what was going on. I had emotionally puked all over him on more than one occasion, venting my anger toward God.

For weeks, Steve had put up with my despicable rants and loved me anyway. He hadn't confronted me or condemned me. He hadn't thrown Scripture in my face. He had simply listened and accepted me right where I was.

It was actually quite irritating. I expected him to blast me. He was a pastor and a seminary student, after all. I figured he had an agenda to "save" me. But for a long time, all he did was show me unrelenting kindness and compassionate love.

For the record, in dealing with a brother or sister who has gone off the rails, there will come a time for "speaking the truth in love" (Ephesians 4:15). But *listening* and *loving* should *always* precede speaking. Of course, we never condone sinful actions, but most people already know the right thing to do—and they may know the Scriptures better than we do. That's why *love* is the key, not shame, judgment, or condemnation.

With me, Steve had earned the right to be heard, and now he was on the other end of the line, saying, "Hey, Kurt, we need to get together."

"Fine," I said. "How about lunch next week?"

"No . . . we really need to get together right away, Kurt."

I relented, "Okay, I can do lunch tomorrow, I guess."

"No, how about right now?"

"Right now? Dude, it's getting late and I need to get to bed." Of course, the fact that I was a bit inebriated didn't help.

"Come on, Kurt, there's a Bob's Big Boy restaurant just down the street from you; meet me there in half an hour."

The week before, I had told Laura I was going to move out and was looking for a place to live. She had remained faithful and patient with me, but she was devastated. We were on the brink of divorce, and frankly I didn't care.

Now Steve calls. *This can't be good*, I thought.

I don't know why I said yes, but I did. And fortunately, because the restaurant was so close to where I lived, I could walk.

What happened over the next couple of hours would take too long to cover in detail. Suffice it to say, it was time for Steve to speak the truth in love. He wasn't self-righteous or harsh. He didn't yell, scream, or spit at me. He did read me the riot act, but he did so humbly and lovingly. He also didn't hold anything back that night as he told me, "You're at the fork in the road, my friend, and you're either going to choose life or choose death."

I knew he was right; and frankly, it made me mad. But it also scared me. I knew he loved me. I knew he would continue to be my friend, no matter what. But I knew I was at the crossroads and it was time to make a decision: return or continue to run?

I may not have cared about a lot of things prior to that night, but I didn't want to live the rest of my life in misery, far from God, and I knew it was up to me to change.

What a Foolish Hunk!

The story of Samson has always fascinated me. Even when I was a kid in Sunday school, the picture of this hunk-of-a-man bringing down the house was one of my favorites. I realize now, of course, that it is actually a tragic tale of a man who let his desires rule him, leading to his ruin. Like me, Samson had some bitterness issues.

In Judges 14–15, Samson falls in love with a Philistine woman. His parents are not happy about this, because no good Jew would marry an idol-loving foreigner. They get married anyway, but through some serious misunderstandings, the new father-in-law thinks that Samson despises his daughter, so he marries her off to another guy while Samson is out of town. What a mess.

When Samson finds out, he goes ballistic (you probably would too) and takes revenge on the Philistines by attaching blazing torches to three hundred foxes tied tail-to-tail in pairs and setting them loose in the Philistines' wheat fields. That is what I call creative revenge!

As the story goes on, Samson continues to viciously slaughter the Philistines. Eventually, however, he is captured and held prisoner by his enemies. But once again, God supernaturally empowers him to defeat and kill a thousand Philistines with the ancient equivalent of a war club (the jawbone of a donkey). Samson then becomes the leader of Israel for the next twenty years. It is quite a story.

Sometime later, Samson winds up with another Philistine woman, named Delilah. She ultimately betrays him as she reveals the secret of his strength to the Philistines. Now Samson the Great is weak and blind, because they've cut his hair and gouged out his eyes, and the Philistines mock him during a ceremony to their pagan god, Dagon.

However, Samson has the final laugh as God empowers him one last time to defeat his enemies, bringing down the supporting pillars of their great temple and destroying them all. Here's the final line in his story: "Thus he killed many more when he died than while he lived" (Judges 16:30).

Samson's story has all the makings of an epic drama: love, violence, and the bad guys getting it in the end. Tragically, it is also a story of a man who once had God's favor and yet allowed his own emotions, bitterness, and foolishness to cost him everything, even his life. I did not want to be that guy.

The Return

After my encounter with Steve that night at Bob's Big Boy restaurant, I headed for home. On the way, I stopped and sat on a rock on a hill overlooking our house and the city. I felt no great emotion. I wouldn't even say I was humbly repentant at that time. I knew, however, that I had to make a choice, and I chose life.

I hadn't talked to God for a long time, but that night I prayed, "God, if you want me back, I'm back. I don't know how to undo all the damage I've done or how to get out of the mess I've created, but I know that my way is gonna kill me, and I don't want to die like this."

From time to time, people say to me, "Pastor, I feel so loved, understood, and accepted by you. Your messages are always filled with truth and grace."

I usually just smile and say, "Ain't God good?" because I know and remember his grace and his goodness. I know what it's like to be consumed by anger, bitterness, and evil and to still hear his voice calling me home. I know what it means to be far from God and to still be unconditionally loved by him and by others. That, my friends, is epic grace.

I was the prodigal son, who found himself wallowing in misery, a misery of his own making, and yet a son profoundly embraced by his Father upon his return. I plumbed the depths of God's grace, and I was embraced by it. Washed by it. Restored by it. Made new by it.

Oh, how he loves me . . .

And oh, how he loves *you*.

The road back to spiritual health and relational healing with my wife was a long one. We met with a counselor many times over the next couple of years. Honestly, there were plenty of setbacks along the way. At a company Christmas party a few months later, I got so drunk that Laura had to drive us home. She wasn't always happy with me, but she was always patient and forgiving. She was (and is) a model of grace and mercy to me.

Sometimes healing is instantaneous, but more often than not, restoration takes time and a lot of hard work. It also takes friends and family who will never give up on you. For me, they seemed to know just when to pat me on the back and when to kick me in the backside. As epic as God's grace is toward us, we also need the grace of others in our journey to restoration.

My friend Joe now pastors more than five thousand people at Life Center in Spokane—which, by the way, is a much better, newer, and cleaner city today. His spin-off, daughter churches—of which mine is one—minister to thousands more. My mom remarried, to a great man who became an awesome stepfather to me. Nathan never experienced any further complications from his jaundice. In fact, he graduated valedictorian of his high school and was a magna cum laude graduate from college. My "difficult" daughter outgrew her colic and became—and still is—a great joy and delight to me. And my dear wife and I just celebrated our thirty-eighth wedding anniversary. We love each other more today than ever.

If God can do this with a guy like me, he can do it with *anyone*. Even you.

4

GOD'S ALGEBRA

See what great love the Father has lavished on us,

that we should be called children of God! And that is what we are!

1 JOHN 3:1

MY PEOPLE HAVE A SAYING.[†] It goes something like this: *You are worth more than the sum of your efforts.* In other words, A plus B does not always equal C. How well you do what you do in life has very little—if anything—to do with your true value to God. Unfortunately, it took me about twenty-five years to learn that lesson.

I grew up in a strange home. We were dysfunctional long before people used that word or even knew what it meant. From the outside, we looked fine. My dad was a pastor. My mom played the organ and could prepare the church bulletin (unspoken requirements for all pastors' wives). The kids were well groomed and well behaved, at least in public. We pretty much lived at church, and I knew all the books of the Bible before I was five. To the casual observer, we looked pretty good.

[†] I've always wanted to say that, even though I don't really have a "people."

But the *real* Bubna home was filled with hostility and fear. Not very spiritual at all. My dad was an angry man with ridiculous standards. He set the bar so high that no one could ever measure up, and when we didn't, he would take the "bar" and beat us with it. It was like living with a wounded and furious bear. My mom was terrified. I was confused, afraid, and often frustrated.

I was confused at first because I knew my dad expected and demanded perfection from his wife and kids, but it was very apparent that he did not abide by the same standard of flawlessness. He was a womanizer. I figured that out by the time I was ten. He drank and smoked, but only at home and only in the secrecy of his bedroom. By the time I was in junior high, he was abusing prescription drugs as well, mostly Valium and sleeping pills. He was physically and emotionally abusive with his children. And the only time I ever made him happy as a kid was when I did something perfectly. Can you see why I was bewildered and discouraged?

Here's what a kid begins to believe about himself in that kind of environment:

1. My value to God and others is based solely on my performance, and
2. My worth is measured by my success.

The really crazy thing about my relationship with my dad is that everything in me longed for his love and approval. I was terrified of him. I sometimes hated him, and I usually avoided him. Yet I wanted nothing more than to please him and to hear him say, "Good job, Son; I'm proud of you!"

Drums Are of the Devil!

My dad wanted me to play the trumpet, so I spent years playing the trumpet just for him—and I was almost always first chair in band because nothing less would do. Frankly, I didn't really like the trumpet. I wanted to play the drums, but according to my dad, rock and roll was evil and drums were "of the devil," and no son of his was going to play something so satanic.

He wanted me to go to the US Naval Academy, so nothing less than A's on my report card was acceptable. So I had a major problem when I hit algebra in ninth grade. I stink at anything beyond pluses and minuses. In my opinion, math should be about numbers, not letters and theorems. I had to basically bribe my algebra teacher just so I could pass the course. You can imagine how disappointed my father was when he saw my grades. I wasn't smart enough to accomplish his dreams for my life.

I remember the day it dawned on me: *You're just an average guy with an average IQ. Nothing special. Nothing to get all excited about.*

I was sitting in algebra listening to Mr. Heinrich (we called him Old Heinie) drone on and on and on, and I had no idea what he was talking about. He was speaking English, I think, but it may as well have been ancient Greek. I was not getting it. I felt very, very dumb. I mean, if you can't do algebra, what is your life worth to the world anyway?

My dad wanted me to play football. But again I had a little problem—*me*. I was about four-foot-nothing until I turned sixteen. Being a small fry is okay if you have some athletic talent. Unfortunately, I had none. I loved the game and still do, but after several years of sitting on the bench, I quit. Another personal defeat. Another disappointment for my dad. Another indication of my general worthlessness. Or so I thought.

I could go on, but I'm sure you get the picture. I desperately wanted my father's unconditional love and approval. I wanted him to be proud of me. I wanted to please him, even though he rarely pleased me. I didn't make him happy very often, and most of the time I felt like a failure. I grappled with deep insecurities because the measure of my worth was performance, and I was an average performer at best.

Regrettably, a lot of people tend to measure their worth and value by what they do or don't do, or by what they have or don't have. They have a little self-voice in their heads, along with the voice of their father or their mother or someone else, telling them that they have to measure up and perform their way into being accepted by others. I know this because I was one of them.

It doesn't help that our culture has pretty screwed-up values as well. We tend to pay a lot more attention to the rich and famous. We treat them as if they are of greater value than the rest of us just because they can hit a ball better or hit a musical note with flair.

Here's what's wrong with all this: Our value as human beings created in the image of God has absolutely nothing to do with our success or lack of success. God loves us and values us because of *who we are* and because of *who he is*. With God, it is not about *what*. It's all about *who*.

Sure, God cares about what we do, but our value to him is not based on our accomplishments—nor is it diminished by our failures. In fact, even when we are at our worst, he loves us and values us. His love is unconditional. Someone once said, "There is nothing I can do to make God love me any more than he already does, and nothing I can do to make him love me any less." Forget the "yeah buts." There is no way around this simple truth. God loves me and I am worth more than the sum of my efforts. Where did I get such a crazy idea? Check this out:

> When we were utterly helpless, Christ came at just the right time and died for us sinners. Now, most people would not be willing to die for an upright person, though someone might perhaps be willing to die for a person who is especially good. But God showed his great love for us by sending Christ to die for us while we were still sinners. ROMANS 5:6-8, NLT

Let those words sink in for a moment: "When we were *utterly* helpless . . . God showed his great love for us . . . while we were *still* sinners." Before we ever did even one thing right. Before we ever loved him. Before we ever had a clue. In fact, when we were utterly clueless, far from God, and messed up, he demonstrated our value to him by sending Jesus to die for us.

You and I mean everything to God. We are the recipients of his unmerited, undeserved, and relentless grace. If you haven't figured it out by now, the words *grace, love,* and *forgiveness* are nearly synonymous. I love the way John R. W. Stott once put it: "Grace is love that cares and stoops and rescues."

Loving People Just Because

A long time ago in a far, faraway place, I worked with a woman named Trish who was pretty messed up emotionally. Trish was mean. Being around her was like being swarmed by angry wasps, and she stung me all the time. Trish hated my guts. I think she hated everybody. I know she hated God. Once, in a moment of foolishness, I asked her if she "knew the Lord." Why do we Christians talk like that?

Anyhow, about five minutes later—after she stopped screaming and swearing at me—I said, "I guess that's a no?" (I told you I was an idiot.) She cranked it up again for the second stanza, and by that time everyone within a hundred feet knew she hated God—and me.

I walked away emotionally bruised and bloodied. It was ugly. By now, I hated Trish. She was scary. I thought she might be the Antichrist.

A funny thing happened on the way to work one day. I drove by Trish on the side of the road as she was trying to fix a flat tire on her car. She was wearing a dress and was kicking and screaming at her car. I knew how her car felt. I'm embarrassed to admit to you that I drove by smiling. I was glad to see her suffering. Sweet revenge. Holy justice. Give her heck, God.

But about a block later, I heard the still, small voice of God saying, *Go back and help her*. Frankly, sometimes I hate that still, small voice. Why doesn't it ever say, *Go back and run her over?* Well, you know what I did. I went back.

As I got out of my car, I said something brilliant to Trish like, "Do you need any help?" *Duhhhh!* She handed me the tire iron and sat down on the curb. Sweating. A lot. And cursing. A lot.

As I was changing her tire, something came over me and I started singing a little praise song. I might have been singing out of fear or nervousness—I'm not sure. But the next thing I knew, Trish was standing right behind me. "What in blazes are you doing?" she asked.

"Changing your tire," I said sheepishly.

"No, you idiot." (She obviously knew me.) "*What* and *why* are you singing?"

Without looking up at her, I mumbled something about God, which neither one of us really understood. I was like a deer caught in the headlights of an oncoming truck. I froze out of sheer terror.

I knew then that I was either going to die as she ripped the tire iron from my hands and beat me to death, or something good was about to happen.

Guess what? Something good happened.

As I turned to look up at her, I noticed she had tears in her eyes. She wasn't wailing and sobbing (though that would have been cool), but she was emotionally moved. My act of kindness had broken through her hard heart.

I wish I could tell you that she fell to her knees right there on the side of the road—in front of God, me, and the whole wide world—and became a Christ-follower. But she didn't. Actually, she just waited for me to finish, got in her car, and drove off without so much as a "thank you." But you know what? That day, she had a God encounter. That day, she saw and heard the love of God—even through a reluctant, resentful, and imperfect vessel like me.

Also that day, I started to love Trish, just like Jesus loves people even when they are mean and ugly to him and they don't deserve it. That is grace in action.

I was beginning to get it.

I was twenty-five years old, and that moment with Trish changed me forever. I had a God encounter too. Through that experience, I began to understand something about my heavenly Father. Something very different from my earthly father.

God loves people just because.

Just because we are amazing creatures created in his image.

Just because we are wounded and broken, and he cares for us beyond belief.

Just because his Son paid the ultimate price to redeem and restore us.

Just because of *who we are*, and not because of what we do.

Shell Game

Several years ago, I was at the Oregon coast staying at a beautiful hotel in Cannon Beach. Every morning, I'd go for a long run along the shore. As I ran, I kept an eye out for any seashells that might be worth keeping.

One particular morning, there were far more shells than usual, so I had more of a walk than a run. At one point, I stopped for the umpteenth time to pick up what looked like a great shell. It was rather big and half buried in the sand. The second I grabbed it, though, I discovered it was only half a shell. The broken part was beneath the surface of the sand. Of course, I was a bit disappointed, but I remained undaunted in my pursuit of the perfect shell. So I dropped the broken piece and resumed my run.

About twenty or thirty feet later, the Lord spoke to my heart: *Go back, grab that shell, and keep it.* That seemed odd, and my immediate response was, "What's the point? It's of no value to me. It's broken!" But before I got those words out of my mouth, I knew this was another one of those God moments for me. Even if it didn't make sense, I knew what I had to do. So I turned around, went back to the spot where I had chucked the shell, and picked it up.

Still thinking it was weird and very perplexing, I then heard the Lord gently add, *You tend to value the whole, but I always value the broken as much as the whole.*

God loves us just because of who we are, not because of what we do, not because we've got it all together, and not because of our efforts—or lack of effort. There is nothing we can do to make God love us any more, and there's nothing we can do to make him love us any less. We are worth more than the sum of our efforts, even if we are broken—maybe *especially* if we are broken. That, too, is epic grace.

My very first grandchild is named Adelle. I love her so much my heart aches sometimes. I love each of my four children and their spouses, but there is something special about grandchildren. It is hard to explain until you've been there.

The first time I held Adelle in my arms is a memory I will never forget. I looked down at her. I talked to her. I told her I loved her and would always be there for her. I cried.

Here is what hit me in that moment. She had no idea who I was. She had no idea how much I loved her. She was clueless. She couldn't understand my words, let alone my heart. She had never done anything for me. She had never given me anything. She had never told me that she loved me. She was only three days old, after all. But none of that mattered to me. I loved her with all my heart, just because of who she was. And I will always love her, no matter what she does or doesn't do.

Listen . . . *that* is the full-of-grace heart of our Father God. That is the way he looks at you and me. Even before we have any idea who he is or how much he loves us. Even before we can understand his words or his heart. Before we have ever done anything for him, he loves us. We don't have to earn his love. We don't have to perform for him. We don't have to do *anything at all* to merit his affection or to be of value to him. He just loves us. Period. That's epic grace.

Why work so hard and struggle so much for something you already have? You have the grace-love of your Father. You really are worth everything to God. In fact, to him, you are priceless.

5

THE CURSE
OF COMPARISON

*There are different kinds of spiritual gifts, but the same Spirit
is the source of them all. There are different kinds of service,
but we serve the same Lord. God works in different ways,
but it is the same God who does the work in all of us.*

1 CORINTHIANS 12:4-6, NLT

WE'VE ALL BEEN THERE, measuring ourselves against the other
guy or gal, and we've all struggled with the haunting question:
Am I good enough, smart enough, strong enough, or skilled
enough to be liked or accepted—let alone loved—for who I am?

My last two years of junior high and my first year of high
school were spent in the frozen wasteland of Hibbing, Minnesota.
It was a one-school town, and everybody knew just about everybody. Junior high can be a tough age for any kid, but imagine
having to swim naked every other day with a hundred other boys.
That's right—*naked*, and I'm not kidding!

Because Minnesota is the Land of 10,000 Lakes, swimming
was a required course in school. In fact, if you didn't pass swimming, you didn't move on to high school. Now imagine the difficulty of dealing with the dampness and probable mold associated
with hundreds of wet swimsuits. There's no way the school wanted

them hung in the PE locker room for nine months, and there was no way we were going to drag them around in our backpacks all day. So the solution was obvious: eliminate the problem by having kids swim in their earth suits.

Every other day, every kid in that school was exposed (literally) to every other kid of the same gender in PE class. The worst part was sitting there buck naked and cold against the pool room wall waiting for roll call, and trying not to look at anything but the ceiling, the water, or the concrete floor beneath you. It was traumatic, to say the least. The minute the teacher blew his whistle, we jumped into the pool like penguins rushing off the ice to avoid a polar bear. The water brought at least a measure of comfort and concealment.

I won't get too graphic here, but I learned early in life that all men (or, in this case, boys) are not created equal. As much as we'd try not to, comparing ourselves to the other naked plebes was inevitable. That could be pretty traumatic for the average junior high boy. Comparison was not only unavoidable, but for skinny little pygmy dweebs like me, it was also painful. I would have done just about anything to change the way I looked.

Nip and Tuck

One of my favorite quotes goes something like this: "Be who you is, because if you is who you ain't, you ain't who you is." I first heard it in a talk by author Brennan Manning (though I don't think it originated with him).[1] This is a powerful truth. The premise is simple: God made us, and he is forming us into the image of his Son, so why would we ever pretend to be someone or something we are not? Just be the man or woman God made you to be.

Stop living behind a mask.

Stop striving to behave as if you're somebody else.

Stop working so hard to change the way you look.

Be who you is, or you is who you ain't.

I did a little research on how much we Americans spend on plastic surgery, and it probably won't surprise you that the number is in the *billions*. Depending on which source you choose to believe, somewhere between $10 and $15 billion is spent every year on face-lifts, enhancements, tummy tucks, and liposuction. Conservatively estimated, an additional $20 billion is spent just on cosmetics.

Okay, for the record, I use deodorant, brush my teeth with whitening toothpaste—and yes, I pluck hair from parts of my body that shouldn't have hair. I'm not advocating that we all walk around as ugly as a hairless Chihuahua, or that we stink like a landfill in August. But seriously, $30 to $45 *billion* every year just to become something we're not? How can we justify this insanity?

Several years ago, I remember reading a newspaper article that said we could solve the world's hunger problem with just $30 billion a year.

According to Living Water International, at least 783 million people in the world do not have access to safe, drinkable water.[2] Almost two million children die every year from diseases caused by unclean water and poor sanitation.[3] Stop and think about that—that's almost 5,500 deaths *per day*. According to estimates, it would take only about $10 billion per year to provide *everyone* in the world with clean, drinkable water.

Eradicate hunger and provide pure water—or primp, pluck, nip, and tuck? Which do you think matters most to God?

Right about now you might be saying, "Dude, back off! Stop laying a guilt trip on me. Capitalism makes the world go round."

I understand. I'm not casting stones at anyone. I sometimes wish I could lipo-suck the fat from my potbelly and still eat all the ice cream I want. Believe me, I know I've got an enormous two-by-four in my own eye, so I'm not trying to gouge the speck out of yours. But maybe something needs to change. Maybe our priorities are off. Maybe we're missing something in our futile attempts to avoid the inevitable. We're all getting old, and eventually we all die ugly—or at least uglier. When's the last time you saw a ninety-year-old whose beauty took your breath away?

So what's at the heart of this issue? Why do we invest billions in body makeovers, Chanel No. 5, and enough Botox to fill an ocean?

One word sums it up: *comparison*. We compare ourselves to everyone else, and we don't like what we see.

Our bellies are too rotund, more like a keg than a Brad Pitt six-pack. Our backsides are too wide compared to Angelina Jolie's. Our wrinkles are too obvious compared to Cher's. Our voice is too squeaky compared to James Earl Jones's. Our hair is too thin compared to Donald Trump's (hard to really know, though, with that comb-over thing). And the list goes on . . .

A mother named Bonnie came to me after church one Sunday. She said she feared she was losing her sixteen-year-old daughter. I thought she meant she was losing her to drugs or booze. In fact, she was watching her daughter waste away because the girl thought she was fat at five-foot-six and a whopping ninety pounds soaking wet. And that wasn't the first time I've had to walk with parents through the nightmare of dealing with a teen-age girl who is anorexic. These young ladies think they have to look like a stick figure to be beautiful. They live with a terror of gaining weight, so they compulsively exercise or purge without concern for what truly matters—their health.

Here's a serious reality you might want to hold on to: Comparison is a trap because it feeds either the beast of pride or the monster of insecurity. Pride comes when we compare ourselves to others and think we are better, smarter, or prettier. Insecurity consumes us when we compare ourselves and focus on our real or imagined insufficiencies. Either way, we lose.

God help us! What will it take for us to figure out that there is *always* someone better and *always* someone worse? What's the point? Really. Why can't we accept who we are—just as God accepts us—rather than getting chewed up in the meat grinder of self-destructive comparisons?

Captain America

Remember dodgeball? For years, just the mention of that word would raise my blood pressure and send me into a dark and gloomy funk. I have the athletic ability of a gnat. As a kid, I was small, slow, and annoyingly untalented. Swimming naked was distressing, but that was only half the story. For me, PE was a daily dose of rejection and embarrassment.

It always happened the same way: The gym teacher, G.I. Joe, would pick the team captains, and the captains would choose their teammates. The captains were always the same two mammoth boys, who had been shaving since fifth grade. These Greek gods were chiseled, and they knew it. They walked with a swagger. They talked with the confidence of a marine drill sergeant. They were destined for greatness because they were endowed with size, speed, and herculean talent.

The team selection process was the most grueling exercise known to boykind. First, Captain America would pick his buddy and fellow all-star, Johnny the Boy Wonder, while eyeing his next potential draft choices. Then Captain Fantastic would select his closest friend, Charles Atlas, and the draft would continue. Back and forth these strapping young captains would go, picking their dream teams with the precision of an NFL scout. Until finally they ended up with the bottom of the barrel, arguing over who *had* to take the pathetic little troll named Bubna.

It was excruciating. I hated every second. The emotional waterboarding I experienced always left me feeling terribly useless and pathetic.

From Bad to Worse

When I got to eighth grade, I had the not-so-bright idea of going out for the school basketball team. I had heard that the players got less homework and sometimes got out of school early. Sounded good to me. There was only one problem: Basketball involves two things that I *never* mastered—dribbling and shooting. In fact, the only thing I did well in basketball was foul people. The school had a no-cut policy, so I was on the team, but that didn't mean they had to put me in the game. Down there at the end of the bench, my worst nightmare came true: I was even worse at basketball than I was at dodgeball. I remember thinking, *How is this possible?*

One day, the coach, who was about as old as Moses, got fed up with our losing record. (I guess I wasn't the only one who lacked skill at basketball.) At the beginning of practice, he sat us all down on the court and told us to keep our eyes open and our mouths shut. He then dragged a ladder out of the corner of the gym and set it up right below the basket. I was getting excited! I thought, *If they start playing this game with a ladder, I might have a prayer of making a basket!* When you are four-foot-nothing, using a ladder seems like a brilliant idea.

I will never forget what the coach did next. Without saying a word, he slowly and carefully climbed to the top of the ladder, holding not one, but two basketballs. When he got to the hoop, huffing and puffing from the first exercise he'd probably had in fifty years, he dropped both balls side by side through the hoop at the same time. We sat there stunned. Who'd have thought that possible? Two regulation balls can fit through that elusive hoop? Simply unbelievable.

With the balls now stuck in the net, the coach wobbled his way back to the floor, looked at us with obvious disgust, and said in a low and rasping voice, "You boys only have to put *one* ball through the hoop at a time! Get your act together or go home!"

After that unforgettable demonstration and inspiring statement, he walked off the court and out of the gym without saying another word. Clearly, if two balls could easily pass through the hoop at one time, it shouldn't be a big deal for us to get at least one ball in every once in a while.

Not knowing exactly what to do next, somebody said, "Forget this! Coach is gone, let's play dodgeball!"

Sigh . . .

Of course, the point of this depressing story is that we learn at an early age to compare, evaluate, and judge our worth based on how we stack up against everybody else.

The guy with the new, expensive European car is obviously better than the guy with the twelve-year-old Buick (that would be me). The hottie with the hourglass figure is the most perfect. The student with the highest SAT score is probably destined for Harvard and eventual greatness. The neighbor with the biggest boat, house, and satellite dish is cool; the rest of us are nothing but feeble wannabes. The pastor with the largest church is gifted and anointed. Tough luck if you're a one-talent guy in a ten-talent world.

Listen, I've got nothing against being your best, doing your best, or even being successful. I'm not lobbying for mediocrity or suggesting that there is something inherently wrong with being a ten-talent guy or gal.

I'm simply arguing that we must stop living in the crippling world of comparison. Let's not get sucked into the realm of pride on the one hand, or devastating insecurity on the other.

When God made you, he knew what he was doing, and he is still in the process of shaping and forming you into the person *he* wants you to be. What's more—news flash!—God likes you now, just the way you are. His epic grace covers not only all your sin, it covers all your inadequacies and weaknesses as well. I love these words from the apostle Paul: "[God] said, 'My grace is all you need. My power works best in weakness.' So now I am glad to boast about my weaknesses, so that the power of Christ can work through me" (2 Corinthians 12:9, NLT).

Somehow, despite our profound awareness of our weaknesses,

we can discover that God's power is all we truly need, and his power is best demonstrated through our deficiencies. If that's not grace, I don't know what is.

The face you see in the mirror every morning may have a nose that's bigger than most or a head with less hair than some. The abilities and gifts you have may not be as stellar as those of others. Your brainpower or communication skills may not be good enough to get you elected president. But God doesn't care about those things. Why should you?

The apostle Paul had to deal with the curse of comparison in the church of Corinth. Apparently, some in that church questioned Paul's legitimacy as an apostle as they compared him to others. Here's Paul's response: "Oh, don't worry; we wouldn't dare say that we are as wonderful as these other men who tell you how important they are! But they are only comparing themselves with each other, using themselves as the standard of measurement. How ignorant!" (2 Corinthians 10:12, NLT).

Using a bit of sarcasm, Paul blasts the whole idiotic idea of comparing ourselves to each other. It's fruitless, pointless, foolish, and ignorant! Mark my words (and his): *No good will come of it.*

Recently, I had coffee with an old friend. He pastors a large congregation in another city. For many years, he has invited me once or twice a year to speak at his church. In fact, I've spoken there so often it feels like a second home to me. I love him. I love the people. I love the church. And I loved speaking there long before it became a megachurch.

Early last year, I once again had the honor of speaking at this fantastic church, and I was scheduled to return there for Thanksgiving weekend. However, a couple of weeks before this return engagement, my friend called and canceled. He said, "We've been working with a young, highly educated and talented pastor in town, and I'm trying to get him to speak at our church once a month or so. I hope you understand, but I'm going to have him speak on Thanksgiving weekend instead of you."

Okay, I'm thinking, *let me get this straight. You're dumping me because I'm old, uneducated, and untalented.* Honestly, that's not what he said, but that's precisely how I felt.

Actually, I understood his reasoning. My friend didn't do anything wrong, and he certainly wasn't trying to hurt me. But I was hurt, nonetheless. Once again, my own insecurities got the best (or worst) of me.

A week or so later, I realized what I had done. I'd fallen into the quicksand of comparison again. In fact, in this one experience I went from insecurity to depression, and it was ugly.

Comparison is a trap.

It will kill our joy.

It will rob us of our peace.

It makes us act foolish and stupid.

It causes dissension and division in the body of Christ.

It creates terrible tension in our relationships with others.

So here's what you need to focus on: Let God use you the way he sees fit to do so. Embrace what he is doing in and through your life. Stop worrying about how you measure up to the guy next door, to the woman in the cubicle down the hall, or to the gifted young leader who replaced you.

Live in the grace that is yours and with the joy that comes from being who God has made you to be. Be who you is, or you is who you ain't!

6

ALL FOR A ROLL IN THE HAY?

If we claim to be without sin, we deceive ourselves and the truth is not in us. If we confess our sins, he is faithful and just and will forgive us our sins and purify us from all unrighteousness.

1 JOHN 1:8-9

WITHOUT QUESTION, my life has been filled with regret, remorse, and a lot of repentance. In fact, I may qualify as a professional repenter. Sometimes it seems as if I've lived a dozen lives and learned a thousand lessons. But here's one I really wish I could have figured out without being such an idiot: *Your future is worth more than any temporary pleasure.* Though it's terribly embarrassing to admit, it turned out to be another lesson I had to learn the hard way.

Too many times, in too many ways, I've lost sight of the future and indulged myself in a momentary and passing pleasure. And I don't mean eating one too many tacos or cookies and paying for it later. I mean outright *sin*—stupid sin that hurt others and hurt me.

I don't remember the first time I blew it (which is a sugarcoated way of saying the first time I blatantly sinned), but I do remember getting an early start.

When I was in seventh grade, we lived in St. Louis. I had a girlfriend named Reba, who was a year ahead of me in school. She was cute and—how do I say it?—well built for an eighth grader, and she was a wild woman. A dream come true for any seventh grade boy with raging hormones.

We never went all the way, but we went way too far, far too often, in her parents' basement rec room. I remember thinking, *How could something so much fun be wrong?*

Still, I felt guilty. I repented over and over. In fact, I must have "gotten saved" a dozen times during that season of my life. In spite of all this, Reba and I would take it too far again the next time we had the chance. Drawn to the basement like rats drawn to peanut butter, we'd end up "recreating" in the rec room.

This went on for a long time, and my guilt got worse and worse. I once woke up in the middle of the night screaming because I'd dreamt that the Rapture happened while Reba and I were fooling around, and I'd been left behind. I remember thinking, *It wouldn't be good if the pastor's son missed the Rapture.*

Fortunately, my family moved to Hibbing about a year later. Reba and I were heartbroken, but I'm sure it kept me from losing my virginity at a very early age.

For a while, Hibbing was better. I kept out of trouble for almost a whole month. But then I met Katrina, the daughter of one of the deacons at the church. She was a year younger, and this time I was the experienced one. She found me irresistible, and *no* was not in either one of our vocabularies.

I was starting to see women as little more than pleasuring

playmates. And unfortunately, I messed around with quite a few girls for quite a few years. I'll spare you the details—because my mother's reading this, after all—but it was bad. Stupid. Really idiotic.

The result, again, was guilt. It consumed me, and I knew I was wrong. I knew that my sin was robbing me of joy, and it's difficult to discover and experience your God-given purpose when you feel like a jerk. Guilt cripples us emotionally and spiritually. I knew I was sinning, but the temporary pleasure still seemed worth the cost. It took me a while to figure out otherwise.

Brother, O Brother!

In Genesis, there is a tale of two brothers, fraternal twins. Their names are Esau and Jacob. Esau was the firstborn by a couple of minutes, and he was the hunk, the hunter, the jock of his day. Esau was his father's favorite.

Jacob was different, "a mild man, dwelling in tents" (Genesis 25:27, NKJV). In other words, Jake was not a hunk, not a hunter, and not a jock. Jacob was a mama's boy. He even liked to cook, for heaven's sake.

One day, Esau came back starving from his latest hunting escapade. Here's the play-by-play:

> [Esau] said to Jacob, "Quick, let me have some of that red stew! I'm famished!" . . .
>
> Jacob replied, "First sell me your birthright."
>
> "Look, I am about to die," Esau said. "What good is the birthright to me?"

But Jacob said, "Swear to me first." So he swore an oath to him, selling his birthright to Jacob.

Then Jacob gave Esau some bread and some lentil stew. He ate and drank, and then got up and left.

So Esau despised his birthright.

GENESIS 25:30-34

What an idiot. Esau despised his birthright; that is, he was indifferent about it. He didn't truly value what he had, so he sold out for a bowl of lentil stew. In pursuit of a temporary pleasure, he lost sight of his future and of what was important.

As the firstborn son, Esau's birthright was a pretty big deal. To begin with, it meant he was guaranteed a double portion of the inheritance. Big bucks! It also meant he would have headship of the family after Isaac's death. He'd be the Big Kahuna. Esau had special status. He was the favored son. He had it all, but that bowl of soup looked and smelled so good, and he was sooooo hungry.

Can you imagine how Esau felt just minutes after being satisfied? A full tummy. A stupid choice. An empty future. I wonder how he explained it to his grandkids.

Thing is, I can imagine how he felt. It's the same way I've felt a hundred times. It feels so good, until you're done.

My youthful indiscretions were a long time ago, but it hasn't been that long since I've sinned. It has been decades since I sinned with a woman, but only a matter of days since my last act of stupidity. According to Jesus, lust counts, right? Different song. Same old tune. Same old results.

Maybe you're one of those people who eventually gets over it. You eventually stop feeling guilty. After a few dozen times, you just don't care anymore. The more you do it (whatever "it" is), the less you are bothered by guilt and shame.

I'm *not* that guy.

When I knew I had sinned, it was like walking around with a rock in my shoe that was constantly irritating and annoying me. Sure, I could put on a happy face and pretend that God and I were tight. That's what self-righteous religious people do. But the stink of my sin was always there, like that bad smell you blame on the dog.

Why do I sell out so easily and for something so temporary?

I know it's hard to believe, but like Esau, I'm a favored son too. And believe it or not, whether you know it or not, so are you. As children of God, we have an amazing birthright, complete with an unbelievable inheritance and all sorts of God-given authority. God has plans for you and me that go beyond our imagination.

You don't believe me? Listen to what Paul writes to the church in Corinth (who were a bunch of messed up folks, by the way): "No eye has seen, no ear has heard, and no mind has imagined what God has prepared for those who love him" (1 Corinthians 2:9, NLT).

God has *big* plans for you and me. In fact, they are so big and so amazing that, without the help of God's Spirit, our pea-size brains can't even begin to picture what they look like.

I wrote this chapter on the island of Kwajalein, a tiny atoll in the Marshall Islands, in the far reaches of the Pacific Ocean. I know what you're thinking: *Life must be rough.* One night, my wife and I took a walk down to the beach before bed. The warm South Pacific wind was blowing through the palm trees. The waves were crashing on the beach. You get the picture. Anyhow, it was an incredible night and pitch black with no moon and no big city lights to hinder our view. When we stopped and looked up, the stars were breathtaking. I've never seen so many, and they were so bright I felt as if I could reach out and touch them. I even tried.

Here's what struck me. God is so much bigger than I am. I'm one small person, on one small planet, in one small part of the universe, and yet he knows me.

He knows my name.

He knows my thoughts.

He knows my past as well as my future.

He knows everything about me.

God created the stars for a purpose, and he created you and me for a purpose too.

As the apostle Paul writes: "We are God's workmanship, created in Christ Jesus to do good works, which God prepared in advance for us to do" (Ephesians 2:10).

We are God's masterpiece, his work of art, and he prepared a whole boatload of good works, in advance, for us to do. He's got a life of adventure planned for us. The word *boring* is not in his vocabulary. But every time we choose to sin, we choose a different path away from his great plans.

Nothing can or ever will change his love for us. We really can't do anything to earn it or lose it. But—and this is a big *but*—our sin short-circuits his plans for us. When we choose to wander off the path, God is not to blame for what we miss. We are.

Let me say it again: It is hard to discover and experience our God-given purpose when we are buried under a ton of self-imposed junk.

Another One Bites the Dust

I've got a buddy named Hank, who for many years was very successful at starting new churches and pastoring. He was my mentor. In fact, much of what I know about leading a church, I learned from him. He is my friend, and I love him like a brother. He had (note the past tense here) a wonderful and attractive wife who loved him and loved Jesus with all of her heart. He pastored a wonderful church in a beautiful city, and the congregation loved him with all of their hearts.

But Hank was an idiot. He lost sight of his future and his God-given purpose, trading it in for a temporary pleasure, an adulterous affair with a woman he let himself fall in love with. It ended up costing him everything. His marriage. His church. The respect and admiration of hundreds and hundreds of people.

What a loss for the Kingdom, all for a roll in the hay.

We've all seen the headlines. The well-known pastor who confessed to having sex with a prostitute. Or another pastor I know of who ran off with a board member's daughter. (That's right—the daughter, not the wife.) Or the former football coach who was accused of having sex with young boys. Too many tragic tales of failure and loss, and they just keep coming. Infidelity cuts across all walks of life.

Sex is good. It's fun. It's amazing! Thank you, God. Thank you, thank you, thank you! But is illicit sex really worth losing everything? Isn't guilt-free sex so much better?

Over the course of a lifelong marriage, sometimes the sex is really good and sometimes it's just okay, but when you're committed to your spouse, your sex life can and should get better with time. When you're comfortable and secure with each other, you can be honest, you can grow, you can adjust. You can experiment and be creative without shame. When you consider all the baggage and shame that comes along with infidelity, guilt-free sex is nothing short of awesome.

Forbidden sex may be exciting at first, but after a while it's still just sex. Why is it so easy to lose sight of the big picture for a temporary pleasure? All for a brief moment that may cost you everything?

Maybe you've been thinking or fantasizing about something bad. Maybe it's something other than sex, and yet you still know it's wrong. Whatever it is, you know without question that it is evil, but the desire for that forbidden pleasure is driving you crazy.

Been there. Done that.

Please listen: *It's not worth it.* It never is. Do not buy the lie. You can choose the right path. You can choose to say *no* to sin and *yes* to God. Tell somebody about your struggle. Bring it into the light. If need be, get counseling from someone you trust who will give you good and wise biblical advice. The temptation to sin loses a lot of its grip on us when we're honest and we get help.

I really wish Hank had called somebody for help.

Like many others—and like me—maybe you've already failed here. Maybe you've gone off the path God planned for you. Maybe you've lost sight of God's future for you just for the thrill of a moment, whether it's sex, drugs, pornography, gambling, too much chocolate, or whatever.

Perhaps it is simply the temptation to secretly hate someone or withhold forgiveness. To cheat "just a little." (Yeah, right.) To stretch the truth. (Uh-huh.) Maybe Satan is weaving a trap to tempt you to leave your spouse and give up on your marriage for no good, holy, or godly reason. Maybe you've sold your unique birthright, and you qualify for the "dumb and dumber" award for foolishness.

Please hear this—it is so important: Epic grace is freely available for everyone. It's bigger than we can possibly imagine, better than we deserve, and strong enough to beautifully transform our broken lives into trophies of God's grace. So embrace it and run to the throne of mercy. It is never too late. You are never too far from God.

I'm pretty sure that the writer of the book of Hebrews was an experienced idiot (meaning he, too, was very familiar with sin). Here's what he writes:

> Nothing in all creation can hide from him. Everything is naked and exposed before his eyes. This is the God to whom we must explain all that we have done.

That's the bad news, but here's the good news:

> We have a great High Priest who has gone to heaven, Jesus the Son of God. Let us cling to him and never stop trusting him. This High Priest of ours understands our weaknesses, for he faced all of the same temptations we do, yet he did not sin. So let us come boldly to the throne of our gracious God. There we will receive his mercy, and we will find grace to help us when we need it.
> HEBREWS 4:13-16, NLT

Jesus understands what you're up against. He's not mad at you. There is no condemnation for those in relationship with God through Christ. None.

But we must come boldly and with confidence to the throne of grace. There we find mercy and epic grace to help us all. His forgiveness is freeing and can be yours right now.

I pray for Hank on a regular basis. He's married now to the "other woman." And believe me, I am not praying from a position of self-righteous superiority. I'm praying as one recovering idiot prays for another. I'm praying because I know that God can redeem and restore Hank. In fact, my last phone conversation with him was very encouraging. God has already begun an astonishing work of restoration in his life.

It's who God is. It's what he does best. He longs to redeem and restore. It's his specialty. And he still has a plan for my friend Hank. Truthfully, no matter what you've done, he still has a plan for you, too.

7

MODERN-DAY PHARISEES

Find out what pleases the Lord.

EPHESIANS 6:10

I HAVE A TATTOO. It's not a skull and crossbones, a naked woman, or anything evil, so relax. But years ago, long before *everybody* had one, I decided to get a tattoo. Maybe because as a kid I thought I'd end up in the navy, or perhaps because I've been a biker for a long time, I've always loved the idea of having some cool body art. Most twentysomethings today don't think anything of it. However, many older and more conservative Christians do.

I'm very aware that tattoos are still a serious issue for many. I've heard their arguments. I know how they feel. I've had well-meaning Christians tell me that they're convinced tattoos are evil and only one step away from the "mark of the beast."

But here's the problem—if I avoided everything that somebody in the church might struggle with, I'd be very boring. Monks would have more fun. And living to please people and avoid their pet peeves can be exhausting.

I love what award-winning author Brennan Manning says about this issue: "Christians have an unfortunate tendency to be preoccupied with the trivial." Frankly, we really do. We judge, we criticize, and we argue and fight over things that just are not that important in the grand scheme of things.

I recognize the potential for abuse of just about anything, so I practice two very important principles: obedience to the Scriptures (don't do what it clearly says *not* to do) and moderation in all things.

For example, it's not okay to hate. The Bible is clear on that one. It's not okay to commit adultery, or kill, or cheat, or lie. It's not okay to get drunk, and it's probably not okay to abuse your body with Twinkies or anything else. Sex within marriage—great! Go for it. Wahoo! Sex outside of marriage—a problem. Using money wisely and in a way that honors God—very good. Loving money and selfishly abusing it—very bad.

Quite a few things are mentioned in the Bible that we are to avoid. No compromise. No question. However, a bunch of things are *not* mentioned in the Scriptures and may not be a problem for God.

You see, more often than not, the real problem isn't with tattoos, or sex, or money. The problem is with our hearts. (More on that later.)

What about causing a brother to stumble? If somebody struggles with my having a tattoo, shouldn't I be concerned? Didn't Paul write something about this issue? Yes, he did. Here's the passage:

> Let us therefore make every effort to do what leads to
> peace and to mutual edification. Do not destroy the

work of God for the sake of food. All food is clean, but it is wrong for a person to eat anything that causes someone else to stumble. It is better not to eat meat or drink wine or to do anything else that will cause your brother or sister to fall. ROMANS 14:19-21

Essentially, Paul is teaching us to put the needs of others before our own. People are worth more than anything we might eat or drink. As the Scripture says, "all food is clean," but it is better not to indulge ourselves if it will cause someone else to fall. Paul makes it very clear in this passage that unity is above all. He also makes it clear that the one struggling is the weaker brother—the unenlightened, uninformed, or unbalanced one. Nonetheless, we are to put our love for others above and beyond our love for anything else. Our liberty must not destroy others.

So how do I handle this and still think having a tattoo is okay?

Here's the deal: More often than not—in fact, 99.99 percent of the time—it's not someone young or uncertain in their faith who questions my tattoo. It's someone self-righteously applying their own standards of propriety. Causing a brother to stumble or fall away from the Lord is not the concern with these exceedingly spiritual folks. Falling off their religious pedestal is the only real risk.

Paul wasn't concerned about upsetting the self-righteous. He was concerned for those who genuinely might be caused to fall away from the faith by our actions. When modern-day Pharisees take issue with me on some debatable issue—majoring on the minors—I might try to correct them, or at least remind them that they must love me and accept me even when they disagree with me. Even if they think I'm the weaker brother on this issue, they still have the responsibility to love me and to put our unity first. According to Paul, they are not allowed to despise, browbeat, condemn, or speak evil of me.

> Accept other believers who are weak in faith, and don't argue with them about what they think is right or wrong. . . . Who are you to condemn someone else's servants? Their own master will judge whether they stand or fall. And with the Lord's help, they will stand and receive his approval. . . .
>
> So why do you condemn another believer? Why do you look down on another believer? Remember, we will all stand before the judgment seat of God. . . .
>
> So then, let us aim for harmony in the church and try to build each other up.
>
> ROMANS 14:1, 4, 10, 19, NLT

Bottom line: It's not just about being right—it's about being relational.

That said, let me be clear about something: Tattoos are *not* the real issue here. They're a hot button for some people and so a good place to launch a discussion, but I'm not promoting body art. I'm actually promoting *obedience*.

You didn't see that one coming, did you?

The real issue is doing what God wants and living to please him and him alone. (Please go back and read that last sentence one more time. Go ahead, I'll wait for you.)

Here's the life lesson: What others think of me is none of my business. What God thinks of me and wants from me is what matters most.

This has been a tough lesson for me to learn. I have a long history of being a people-pleaser. Remember, I struggled all of my childhood to please my dad, so I've had years of practice. I really wrestled with coming out of the closet about my tattoo. It would be easier—and maybe smarter—to just not talk about this stuff. People-pleasers tend to avoid controversial subjects.

But maybe it's time for the church to stop majoring on the minors and to stop judging others so ruthlessly.

Maybe it's time for us to love and accept one another the way God does.

Maybe it's time to trust that God is able to speak to people about their lives, without my judgmental two cents' worth.

And maybe it's time for me to concern myself with confessing and surrendering the two-by-fours in my own eyes rather than gouging at the speck of sawdust in someone else's.

Party in the Cul-de-sac

About eight years ago, we moved into a nice neighborhood with nice yards and nice cars and nice kids. My wife and I wanted to get to know our neighbors. We wanted to love them and befriend them the way Jesus would. But at first we weren't sure how. It's a little awkward to invite people you don't know over for dinner. Besides, the rumor got out pretty quickly that I was a pastor, and pastors sometimes make people nervous.

I've decided from now on to start telling people I'm a *relational consultant*. That sounds cool and intriguing and nonthreatening, right? But on my street it was too late. The word was out, and most saw me as a potential hazard to avoid.

One day, I noticed a group of neighbors out in the cul-de-sac.

They were sitting in lawn chairs, watching their kids play in the street and drinking beer. I decided to grab a lawn chair and join them—and it was great.

I think Jesus would have done the same thing. After all, look at where we find him in the Gospel of Mark:

> While Jesus was having dinner at Levi's house, many tax collectors and sinners were eating with him and his disciples, for there were many who followed him. When the teachers of the law who were Pharisees saw him eating with the sinners and tax collectors, they asked his disciples: "Why does he eat with tax collectors and sinners?"
>
> On hearing this, Jesus said to them, "It is not the healthy who need a doctor, but the sick. I have not come to call the righteous, but sinners."
>
> MARK 2:15-17

Obviously, this was a major problem for the Pharisees, who were the ultra–right wing religious folks of Jesus' day. They wouldn't have been caught dead with those people. They were far more concerned about appearances and pleasing men than they were about pleasing God. Jesus, however, was all about doing the will of his Father. He was all about loving the lost and the broken. His reputation meant nothing to him. Pleasing the Father was the only thing that mattered: "I have come down from heaven not to do my will but to do the will of him who sent me" (John 6:38).

And what was the will of his Father? Jesus said, "The Son of Man came to seek and to save the lost" (Luke 19:10).

There is no doubt in my mind that Jesus would have joined his neighbors in the cul-de-sac. He would have liked them, and they would have liked him too.

I really enjoy my neighbors. Even the ones who are far from God. Frankly, I would rather party with them than hang out with some of the self-righteous Christians I know.

What about Bob?

Sadly, one of those Christians was also one of my neighbors. Bob's a good guy. He works hard for a living. He's got a great family. He goes to a good church. But he's also a little pushy about his faith. He means well, and I'm not trying to judge him or throw him under the bus, but at times Bob acts like a modern-day Pharisee.

Unfortunately, I understand Bob all too well. I've been just like him. Self-righteousness comes easy for me. (I've noticed it comes easy for a lot of people.) In years gone by, I had the same condemning, judgmental attitude myself. I'm right, you're wrong. I'm good, you're b-b-b-bad to the bone.

Bob is one of those guys who would rather tear off his lips than have a drink. You know, the whole "if your eye causes you to sin, pluck it out" thing. The first time he saw me hanging out with the beer-drinking neighbors was pretty tough on him. I got the evil eye, the look of disgust, the shaking head, and clucking tongue of shame. He was shocked and appalled. (I think those words mean the same thing but I want to emphasize the point.) It was ugly, and for some reason I felt sort of cheap and sleazy, like a polyester suit at the prom. (Whoa . . . flashback to a very bad day.)

But here's a reality check. Jesus was the only one to ever live a perfect life. If anybody had the right to judge others, it was him. But here is what he said about this whole judging thing: "Do not judge, or you too will be judged. For in the same way you judge others, you will be judged, and with the measure you use, it will be measured to you" (Matthew 7:1-2).

The most famous verse in the Bible has to be John 3:16: "For God so loved the world . . ." But do you remember verse 17? It goes like this: "For God did not send his Son into the world to condemn the world, but to save the world through him."

Why aren't we more like Jesus? Why do so many Christians tend to be so doggone judgmental? Why am *I* that way so often?

The transformation from modern-day Pharisee to grace-filled follower of Jesus is a challenging one for many of us. It's difficult to let go of our pet peeves, but that's the first step. Most of us are extremely opinionated (myself included), but we must learn to love others more than we love being right.

We've been told so many times to be *in* the world but not *of* it that we worry about compromising our witness. I also know that sin is a slippery slope and how easy it is to end up someplace we never intended to go. All legitimate concerns, I agree.

However, as we become more like Jesus, we will have more of his heart for the lost and disenfranchised in our culture. We will worry less about our own reputation and more about building bridges to those who are far from God. Living as ambassadors of God's epic grace is messy at times and requires us to embrace people who are covered in the filth of their sin without any self-righteous judgment on our part.

The transformation starts in our hearts and begins with a simple yet powerful prayer: "Jesus, make me more like you."

One of my heroes is a pastor and author named Jerry Cook. Years ago, he wrote a book titled *Love, Acceptance and Forgiveness*. It is one of the best books I've ever read and continues to be relevant for the church thirty years later. Jerry writes:

> People need to be saved and brought to wholeness
> in every area of their lives. But before there can be
> a coming to wholeness, certain guarantees must be
> made to them. Otherwise they will not risk opening
> themselves to us enough to receive healing.
>
> The minimal guarantee we must make to people
> is that we will love them—always, under every
> circumstance, with no exception. The second guarantee
> is that we will accept them totally, without reservation.
> The third thing we must guarantee people is that no
> matter how miserably they fail or how blatantly they
> sin, unreserved forgiveness is theirs for the asking with
> no bitter taste left in anybody's mouth.[4]

Love means accepting people the way they are—for Jesus' sake. If we're too holy to allow people to blow smoke in our faces, then we're holier than Jesus was. Jesus hung around sinners. He didn't isolate himself in the synagogue. In fact, he mixed with sinners so much that the self-righteous Pharisees got upset about it. Isn't that fantastic? Jesus spent his time with dirty, filthy, stinking sinners. And when those kinds of people find someone who will love and accept them, you won't be able to keep them away.

I want to be more like Jesus and more like Jerry.

I appreciate the way Eugene Peterson puts the problem

with religiosity in his introduction to Galatians in *The Message*: "When men and women get their hands on religion, one of the first things they often do is turn it into an instrument for controlling others."

I've spent way too much of my life being controlled by others, worrying about what they think of me. But what others think of me is none of my business. What God thinks and wants matters most. I didn't even start to figure this one out until I was almost thirty years old.

Stop Striving

In 1989, I worked for a bank in West Palm Beach, Florida. There was a woman named Rita who worked for me. In a word, she was tough. She didn't take garbage from anybody. She also thought she should have my job, and she was probably right. I really wanted her to like me, and I wanted to keep her happy, so I did my best to give her what she wanted, when she wanted it. But conflict was always on the horizon.

There was also a woman named Sybil working for me, and she was no pushover either. She was a strong woman. I'm pretty sure she could have crushed me with one hand and without much effort. Sybil didn't want my job—in fact, I don't think she wanted *her* job—but it was obvious to her that I was giving Rita preferential treatment. Man, did that push her hot buttons.

What a mess. And of course I handled the situation like an idiot. I'd do something to keep Rita off my back, and Sybil would be in my office, screaming, two minutes later. So I'd either try to undo what I had done for Rita or I'd try to bribe Sybil to shut her up, or both. I was miserable. I was failing at one of my most important life missions: keeping people happy and pleasing them at all costs.

One day, after writing my eighth resignation letter, I went up to the roof. I didn't go there to jump, although that might have seemed like an option at the time. I went there to deliver checks to the helicopter that came every day for pickup. I was standing on the roof, complaining to God about my life. I held him responsible for my predicament. Why is it we so often blame God for our choices?

As clearly as I've ever heard God speak to my heart, he said, *Stop striving to please others. Start pleasing me and only me.* It was like a bolt of lightning had hit me—which, by the way, is extremely possible in Florida, especially when one is standing on top of a building. God was in my face about something that was a deep-seated part of my character. Stop striving to please others. What does that look like? Start living for an audience of one. Is that *really* possible?

The helicopter came and went, but I stayed up on the roof for a while. Thinking. Praying. Crying.

"God, I can't do this on my own. I've spent way too much of my life living to make everybody else happy. Help me. Please help me."

I went back down to the lions' den. Nothing had changed in my circumstances, but a whole lot had changed in me. Sometimes God turns a light on in our darkness and we see what we've never seen before. I realized how foolish I'd been trying to keep everybody happy. Because people-pleasing was a deep-seated part of my personality, I literally had to remind myself daily to endeavor to please God first and foremost. In fact, for months, I carried a little note in my wallet that read: "It's not about you; it's not about them; it's all about him!"

That day, on a rooftop in south Florida, I began a new part of my journey with God. That day I decided to focus more—a lot more—on pleasing him than on pleasing others. I'm here to tell ya, it is a radical and freeing way to live. It is also much simpler. "God, what do *you* want? What would *you* do? How can I please *you* first and foremost in my life?"

I still struggle sometimes. I'll probably wrestle with this at least a little bit for the rest of my life. But I tend to think about God *first* now, and it's a much healthier way to live.

I eventually got better at dealing with Rita and Sybil. Instead of juggling their demands—and getting stressed out in the process—I evaluated their wants and wishes in light of God's desire for them and for me. It's funny how things come into focus when your attention is where it should be, on an audience of one.

What others think of me is none of my business. What God thinks and wants always matters most.

By the way, did I mention that some of my beer-drinking neighbors are now coming to our church?

8

"MOMMY, WHY DOES HE WALK FUNNY?"

If I must boast, I will boast of the things that show my weakness.

2 CORINTHIANS 11:30

MY FRIEND AND I WERE WALKING to the beach together. He's a studly sort of fellow, Dutch-Indonesian, with dark skin, dark hair, and well-defined muscles. The kind of guy I usually hate walking next to anywhere, let alone on the beach half naked.

As a child, my friend suffered from polio and one of his legs was affected. He walks with a bit of a limp. As we passed a mom and her little girl who were getting slathered up with sunscreen, the little girl said, "Mommy, why does that man walk funny?"

I don't think my buddy heard her, or if he did, he didn't acknowledge it. The mom, of course, was horrified and stuck her sunscreen-slathered hand over her daughter's mouth, with a look that said, *Say one more word and you'll never talk again!*

Kids—they're so honest. Sometimes it's embarrassing, but I usually find their honesty refreshing. However, what the little girl didn't see is that I walk with a limp too. Not a physical one, but an emotional and spiritual one. In fact, the older I get, the more I realize that a lot of people walk through life with a limp, and it's okay. In fact, one of the most important lessons I've learned in life is never to trust anyone who doesn't walk with a limp.

You see, people with a limp tend to be people with humble hearts. They've been broken. They've lost something. The struggles and hurts of their lives have made them sensitive to the struggles and hurts of others. Whatever part of them may have been self-righteous is gone now. That makes them approachable. It makes them real. It makes them trustworthy. There's something in the way they look at you, and in the way they talk to you, that brings you comfort rather than condemnation. They are grace-driven people. Some of them epically so.

Honoring My Dad

A few years ago, a woman challenged me after hearing me share about my dad in a message. She felt I was not honoring him. Honor is a big deal in the Scriptures. Honoring our parents is important.

I shared with her about a conversation I'd had with my dad a few years before he passed away. At that time, my dad was attending our church. It's a little weird having your father in the congregation listening to you after years of being in the congregation listening to him; but he was always encouraging to me.

In preparing a message one week, I decided I wanted to tell a family story. It was similar to some of what I've shared about my dad and our family in this book. Not very flattering. In fact, somewhat embarrassing.

I knew I needed to talk to my dad first. I didn't want to hurt him, so I gave him a call.

"Hey, Dad, I'm talking about trials this Sunday, and I wondered how you'd feel if I was pretty honest—in fact, brutally honest—about our family? More specifically, how would you feel if I talked about *you*?"

I will never forget my father's words to me. He said, "Son, if God can use my past and my mistakes to help someone avoid what I did—preach on!"

The last few years of my dad's life were his best. He and I were finally close. He was drug-free and spiritually the healthiest he had ever been in his life. In the end, I had the dad I had always wanted.

His journey, however, was long and hard. By the time my dad was fifty-five, he had lost just about everything of value in his life.

- He had a dead-end job that required long hours and lots of driving on Southern California parking lots (also known as highways).
- He'd been married and divorced three times. Twice from his second wife.
- His only daughter would have nothing to do with him.
- He was bankrupt.

One day, he was on the job in a small truck driving in a bad rainstorm when his vehicle went out of control, and he hit the guardrail at about 60 mph. Though he survived the accident, he broke his back, which led to multiple surgeries over the next couple of years and a total of fourteen weeks in the hospital.

Even after the surgeries, he was unable to stand up straight or walk without pain—and that lasted the rest of his life.

I had seen my dad go through many other seasons of difficulty, and usually he just got worse spiritually and emotionally. Everyone around him knew he was his own worst enemy. Nothing and no one ever seemed to get through to him. But this time, with a broken back and a broken life, he finally came to his senses. He finally truly humbled himself and cried out to God. The last few years of his life were his best years because he finally stopped running from God.

Literally on his deathbed, dying of cancer at just sixty-three years of age, he again looked me in the eye and said, "Son, let the first part of my life be an example and reminder to you of what *not* to do, and let my last few years be a model to you of obedience and faith."

Every time I tell a story about my dad, I honor him, because it was his wish to see others spared the tragic results he went through. He was a broken and humbled man. My dad walked with a limp his last few years on this planet, and it was a beautiful thing to see.

Like Father, Like Son

By now, you might be thinking, *Why is Kurt being so hard on himself? Surely he hasn't been quite the idiot he makes himself out to be.* But I have been, and you're not even halfway through the book yet. Yet my heart is just like my daddy's. If anyone can learn something from my mistakes, then maybe something good can come from all this. I walk with a limp, too, and it's okay.

In his autobiography, Martin Luther King Jr. writes, "God

can transform man's weakness into his glorious opportunity."[5] God can take our weaknesses, our past, and even our failures and use them for his glory. It's what he does best. He redeems. He restores. He takes whatever we give to him, and he turns it into something good for us and others. The key is giving it up to him, and then letting go of our past, as we learn to live in God's grace and love.

Maybe you've read this passage of Scripture before:

> We know that God causes everything to work together for the good of those who love God and are called according to his purpose for them. For God knew his people in advance, and he chose them to become like his Son, so that his Son would be the firstborn among many brothers and sisters. And having chosen them, he called them to come to him. And he gave them right standing with himself. And having given them right standing, he gave them his glory.
>
> ROMANS 8:28-30, NLT

God causes *everything*—even our idiotic mistakes—to work together for the good of those who love him. As the apostle Paul says, "God knew his people in advance." That is, he knew what we would do. His ultimate goal for us is that we become "like his Son." That's why he gave us "right standing with himself." That's why he promised us his glory.

Please go back and read the passage from Romans 8 again. Read it slowly and out loud.

It's astounding, isn't it? It's almost too good to be true. It truly is amazing grace.

I don't know where you've been or what you've done, but I do know this—God can fix anything surrendered to him. You'll probably walk with a limp for the rest of your life. That's okay. Welcome to the club. But God can use even your lameness to bring something beautiful out of the ashes of your despair.

And in This Corner . . .

Remember our friend Jacob, the brother of Esau? When last we saw him, his colorful past was about to catch up with him, or so he thought. He had left home in fear of his brother after tricking Esau out of his birthright. He'd been gone for twenty years or so, and now God shows up and tells him, "Go back to the land of your fathers and to your relatives, and I will be with you" (Genesis 31:3).

"Good idea, God. Why didn't I think of that? You've got to be kidding, right? Esau's gonna kill me!"

But Jacob heads for home. Along the way, he finds out that his brother is coming to meet him with four hundred men!

Jacob's response? "Great fear and distress" (Genesis 32:7). You'd react that way too. Don't forget, Esau was a big boy with a big score to settle.

Then Jacob does what any smart person does when trouble is about to start. He prays.

> Then Jacob prayed, "O God of my father Abraham,
> God of my father Isaac, LORD, you who said to me,
> 'Go back to your country and your relatives, and I will
> make you prosper,' I am unworthy of all the kindness
> and faithfulness you have shown your servant. I had

only my staff when I crossed this Jordan, but now
I have become two camps. Save me, I pray, from
the hand of my brother Esau, for I am afraid he
will come and attack me, and also the mothers with
their children.   GENESIS 32:9-11

It seems pretty obvious to me that Jacob is a different man. He
says to God, "I am unworthy of all the kindness and faithfulness
you have shown your servant." Somewhere along the way, Jacob
was humbled. He's now a broken and contrite guy.

Nonetheless, there was a bit more God wanted to do in
Jacob's heart. It's a wonderful story.

That night Jacob got up and took his two wives, his
two maidservants and his eleven sons and crossed the
ford of the Jabbok. After he had sent them across the
stream, he sent over all his possessions. So Jacob was
left alone, and a man wrestled with him till daybreak.
When the man saw that he could not overpower him,
he touched the socket of Jacob's hip so that his hip was
wrenched as he wrestled with the man. Then the man
said, "Let me go, for it is daybreak."

But Jacob replied, "I will not let you go unless you
bless me."

The man asked him, "What is your name?"

"Jacob," he answered.

Then the man said, "Your name will no longer be
Jacob, but Israel, because you have struggled with God
and with men and have overcome."

Jacob said, "Please tell me your name."

But he replied, "Why do you ask my name?" Then he blessed him there.

So Jacob called the place Peniel, saying, "It is because I saw God face to face, and yet my life was spared."

The sun rose above him as he passed Peniel, and he was limping because of his hip. Therefore to this day the Israelites do not eat the tendon attached to the socket of the hip, because the socket of Jacob's hip was touched near the tendon. GENESIS 32:22-32

All of his life, Jacob had struggled with God and with men. Now, he's in a sumo wrestling match with an unidentified man—who some scholars believe was a pre-incarnate manifestation of Jesus Christ. In other words, he's wrestling with God. Way to go, dude!

Jacob, always the opportunist, refuses to give in until God blesses him. And what was the blessing God gave him? A new name. More than that, a new identity.

"You'll no longer be known as Jacob, the conniving deceiver. From now on, it's Israel—*one who strives with God and yet prevails"* (my paraphrase).

Jacob struggled with his brother, with his father, with his father-in-law, and probably with his wives. (Keep in mind that he had been tricked into marrying the sister of his beloved Rachel, and then Rachel had been unable to conceive a child for years. That had to present some interesting challenges.) Jacob struggled with God, too. But things were different now because *he* was different now.

Notice here what else happened. Jacob's hip was "wrenched"

in the struggle. God hit him below the belt—and that had to hurt. The common belief is that Jacob, now called Israel, walked with a limp for the rest of his life. It was a constant reminder to him of his encounter with God.

By the way, this limping man became the father—and namesake—of an entire nation.

How did things turn out with Esau? "Esau ran to meet Jacob and embraced him; he threw his arms around his neck and kissed him. And they wept" (Genesis 33:4).

God can fix anything and anyone.

He took an emotionally limping murderer named Moses and made a great leader out of him. He took a limping, sexually exploited woman named Rahab and put her in the lineage of the Messiah. He took a limping and despised tax man named Matthew and made an apostle out of him. He took a self-righteous religious bigot named Saul, knocked him on his derriere, gave him a new name (Paul) and a thorn in the flesh (which served as a limp), and had him write more than half the New Testament as he spread the Good News about Jesus throughout the Mediterranean.

God takes the arrogant and the proud and he humbles them for a greater purpose. Somehow, somewhere along their journey, God touches their "hip." He changes them from the inside out, and then he blesses them beyond belief.

I know—I've wrestled with God, and I walk with a limp too.

9

YOU DON'T WANT TO READ ABOUT THIS

The LORD is close to the brokenhearted;

he rescues those whose spirits are crushed. . . .

He heals the brokenhearted and bandages their wounds.

PSALMS 34:18; 147:3, NLT

SEXUAL ABUSE. Two of the ugliest, harshest, and most vile words in the English language. Whether we mention it in public, as I have as a speaker, or in private conversation, the words always raise our blood pressure. They produce an immediate reaction in most, and pain in many.

I really don't want to write this chapter, but I must. You may not want to read it, but I think you need to.

One night a few years ago, my wife and I were watching a couple of shows on television. Both of the programs were about horrible sexual abuse and other related crimes. As I sat there, disgusted and angry at what I was seeing, something broke loose in me and I came face-to-face with something I had never told anyone.

Once, when I was a young boy, I was sexually abused.

I went to first, second, and third grade in the wet, sleepy little town of Renton, Washington. Today, Renton is a huge and very developed suburb of Seattle, but back in the early 1960s it was far from that. We lived in a house surrounded by acres of woods, and it was a dream location for any young wannabe Daniel Boone like me.

I spent my summer days building tree forts and wandering through the woods with a coonskin hat, a dull hatchet tucked in my belt, and my BB gun in hand. It was a time in America when most kids ran free in their neighborhoods without fear. Most of the time, my folks had no idea where I was or what I was doing, and nobody worried about it.

I don't think it was as much a time of innocence as it was a time of ignorance. Horrible things happened, but the community at large lived blissfully unaware of the evil just down the street or just down the hall in untold numbers of homes.

According to the experts, sexual abuse has affected 15 to 25 percent of women and 5 to 15 percent of men in North America. Some think the actual numbers are much higher, or at least on the high end of this scale. What it boils down to is that at least one in four or five women and one in ten men have suffered, at some level, the devastating impact of abuse. Whatever the numbers, the reality of sexual abuse is appalling.

As a pastor, I've sat with many women, and with more men than you would imagine, and I've heard their heartbreaking stories of abuse. Frankly, I've heard things that have literally made me sick, and I've had to deal with mental images that are almost too much to bear. And that's just from *hearing* these stories, not living through them as these people have.

I usually sit there wondering in dazed confusion, *How could a parent (or relative or clergyman or teenage babysitter) do that to a child? What corrupt, twisted, broken part of their humanity could cause them to violate and damage someone so young and innocent?*

My own story is not something I suppressed for years. I had just never seen it in the context of sexual abuse. Compared to the horrific stories of repeated and unspeakable atrocities I'd heard about in the lives of others, what happened to me seemed almost unimportant.

It was 1963—the year the Beatles released their second album in Great Britain—and I was in first grade. Martin Luther King Jr. issued his "Letter from Birmingham Jail." America's fight in Vietnam hadn't really started, but things were heating up in that part of the world. And John F. Kennedy was assassinated in the fall of that year.

As kids, we were very untethered during that era. We'd run from yard to yard and house to house without a second thought or a sliver of concern for our safety. It was like we lived in a big sandbox. As long as we were in our familiar world, we didn't fear anything or anybody (except maybe the bogeyman who lived in my closet).

There was an older boy who lived in our neighborhood. He was twice my size and twice my age. I don't remember his first name—everybody called him Junior—but I do remember that his dad had some serious problems. My mom once told me that the father was an alcoholic, but as a kid, that didn't mean much to me. I just knew that this boy was dreadfully afraid of his dad.

My friend didn't like Daniel Boone, which I thought was weird. He didn't want to wear a cool frontier hat, fight Indians, or build forts, either. He did, however, like to steal things. I'm pretty sure he stole my BB gun—though it could have just been that my mother got rid of it because she hated guns, which I also thought was weird.

A Not-So-Good Walk in the Woods

One day, when my friend and I were out exploring in the woods behind my house, he asked me if I wanted to play a new game. Even though I thought it was strange that he didn't want to do the things I loved to do, there was a part of me that wanted to be accepted by this older, stronger boy.

"Sure," I said. "What do I have to do?"

Before I knew it, he had spread out a blanket he'd brought along, I was taking my pants off, and he was touching me. I honestly don't remember what happened next. I've probably blocked that part of the experience out of my memory. But I do remember how I felt afterward.

This whole thing happened about fifty years ago, but I can still recall a mix of emotions. On the one hand, it felt good. It was pleasurable. Arousal is arousal and we were created to respond to sexual stimulation. On the other hand, I felt guilty. Even as a child who was clueless about sex, I somehow knew that what he was doing was wrong. Good to feel. Bad to experience. So from that day on, I avoided that kid and we never went for a walk in the woods together again.

I now know that the technical and legal description of what happened to me is child-on-child sexual abuse. This is when a preadolescent child is sexually abused by one or more other children or adolescent youths, and no adult is directly involved.

Here's something else I now know—sexual abuse is still sexual abuse, no matter who does it or how old the offender is.

One of the reasons I've never talked about this publicly before now is that my experience was only one time, with another child, and not really all that traumatic for me.

Another reason why I've hesitated is that I've never wanted to be defined by what has happened to me. There's probably some foolish pride there, but it's hard to admit to being a victim of sexual abuse.

Of course, a small part of me also fears what others might think. We all know how victims sometimes become victimizers and abusers themselves. I'm sure my concern about what others might believe or assume has contributed to my silence. The last thing I'd ever want is for a parent to be concerned about what I might do to their child. I love kids in the holiest and healthiest of ways. To be seen, even for a moment, as a potential child abuser would kill me.

Here's why I'm willing to take the risk of public disclosure on this issue.

We have to talk about it.

We have to deal with it.

We have to remove the fear and stigma that adds to the emotional trauma of the abused.

We have to encourage the abused *and* the abusers to come into the light of God's power and healing.

We have to tell the victims, "You don't have to live in shame. You no longer need to hide in fear. You can be whole again. You can be free. You don't have to carry that burden anymore."

We also need to tell the victimizers, "You too can be forgiven and live free." This is the heart of epic grace—it's grace for all.

Scandalous Grace

Not long ago, a man in his late fifties came up to me after one of our church services. I had talked about sex that day, and I could tell he was extremely troubled. I expected to hear him say that he disagreed with me about one of the points in my message. When I talk about sex, it often stirs the pot, and I occasionally get some heated e-mails and a verbal enema or two.

What he said, however, broke my heart. He said, "Pastor, I was abused for years as a child, and when I grew up, I became an abuser. I was busted, and I paid my debt to society, but I've never forgiven myself or believed God could ever forgive me either."

His head was held low and his eyes were locked on the carpet beneath his feet. This was a man consumed by guilt and shame. I gently put my hands on his shoulders, asked him to look me in the eye, and said, "Forgiveness is God's specialty. There's nothing too big for him and no life beyond his power to redeem, restore, and renew."

We all have strong emotions when it comes to the issue of abuse. Whether we've personally been abused or not, we ache over this all-too-common problem in our world. There are many who feel relegated to the scratch and dent shelf of life because of sexual sin.

So what are we to do? How should we then live in a world so broken and dark? What would God have us do with both the victims and the perpetrators of such heinous sins?

You already know the answer, don't you?

We extend grace. A grace that is seen through selfless acts of kindness. A grace that is heard through gentle words of healing. A grace that is experienced through unconditional and unmerited love toward one another. A grace so amazing that it covers all our sins and all the sins against us.

Certainly we don't ignore or excuse the sins committed against us, any more than God ignores ours. But we can't stay stuck there either. And the secret to getting unstuck is to forgive as we have been forgiven, to love as we have been loved, and to show others the extravagant and outrageous favor that God has shown to us.

Somewhere along our path, we take ownership of our junk, embrace the Cross for our sins, and then move on in God's strength and with his ever-present help.

Somewhere along the journey, we forgive those who have sinned against us. It's not easy. We'd rather look for some very large millstones to hang around their necks and very deep oceans to drop them into.

But grace is epically scandalous. It chooses to let go of personal judgment, hatred, and bitterness. It chooses to love even the worst offense and the worst offender.

And sometimes, when we have a friend or family member who has suffered the unspeakable, the best thing we can do for them is extend grace too.

They may act out.

They may have some unresolved emotional baggage.

They might be terrified of being rejected by you—not for what they've done, but for what has been done against them.

They may be hiding behind a mask of some sort—appearing to be the life of the party on the outside, but tragically broken and confused underneath. Or they may be cold, distant, and detached because the ache of sin robs them of true joy.

One of my dearest friends was sexually abused as a child.

She is a strong, capable, and creative woman—an amazing person by anyone's standards. The tragedy of her abuse, however, haunted her most of her life. No matter how well she did or how successful she became, in her mind she never measured up. As a result, for years she treated people with the harshness and callousness of a drill sergeant, not allowing anyone to get too close to her heart.

What can we do for the broken people all around us?

Love them. Affirm and accept them. Let them see in our eyes the untamed and epic grace of Jesus. And then show them as often as we can the grace of God through simple acts of love and goodness. Grace is better seen than heard.

At times, I've wondered what became of Junior. Looking back, I realize it's possible he was sexually abused by his alcoholic father. In any case, I hope that he has come to know the God of grace that I know. And I hope he has experienced the freedom that comes through forgiveness and the joy of redemption. That's my prayer for him.

I weep for those who have suffered under the dark shadow of abuse for so long. And I pray for the day when there will be no more tears, no more sorrow, and no more sin.

Until that day, God's grace is the answer.

It always has been and always will be.

10

THIS LITTLE PIGGY WENT TO MARKET

If you need wisdom—if you want to know what
God wants you to do—ask him, and he will gladly
tell you. He will not resent your asking.

JAMES 1:5, NLT

LET'S BE HONEST—nobody likes it when the preacher starts talking about money. (You just thought about skipping this chapter, didn't you?) It's okay. I understand. But I'm sure you'll want to hear about my idiotic mistakes with moolah. Hang in there—this could be fun.

I like to shop. There, I said it. I love the crowds and the smells and the windows filled with great stuff. I really love Nordstrom. I've even thought about working there on the side just to get an employee discount. I could go shopping every day and never get tired of it. For me, it's the thrill of the hunt.

I have just one itsy-bitsy problem: Shopping means spending money, and it is sometimes money I do not have. Fortunately, I'm married to an Irishwoman who loves to save and hates to shop. As you can imagine, this has been the source of some planetary-sized battles between us. Unlike Adam, I've never been able to blame "the woman God gave me" for any of the financial messes in our marriage.

Once upon a time, in a far, faraway place called Florida, I got the brilliant idea to buy an RV. Everybody needs one, or so I thought. They are enjoyable and great for the fam. There is nothing wrong with owning some fun-on-wheels. Really, it's okay; if you own one, don't feel guilty. God still loves you. You are still going to heaven. You're special. However, being able to afford it and make the payments is generally a good idea.

My wife kindly asked two very important questions. First, why do we need this? And second, how are we going to pay for it? Man, she can tick me off sometimes.

Why do we need this?

That's like asking why Edmund Hillary needed to climb Mount Everest. Or why Amelia Earhart needed to be the first woman to fly across the Atlantic. Or why another Hillary ever wanted to be president.

What a stupid question.

"Why do we need this?" she asked.

I countered, "Are you kidding?"

Here was my profound reasoning (and trust me, I can rationalize just about anything): We were about to move back to Southern California. We had four kids, a new Rottweiler puppy, a cat, several pet rodents, and an assortment of other creatures too numerous to mention. What better way to travel three thousand miles through some of the ugliest country in the world than in the comfort of our home away from home? It would be like our very own ark. Plus, we would save lots of money by not needing to stay in motels or eat in restaurants. A brilliant strategy. Impeccable logic. A faultless plan.

In case you're curious, that plan didn't work out so well. Our RV was a converted van. It barely slept two comfortably, let alone two adults and four kids. Now imagine driving five days with four fighting kids, an incontinent puppy, and a cat trying really hard to get to the pet rats.

It was a nightmare. I might be exaggerating a bit about the animals, but you get the picture. Without a doubt, it ranks right up there with one of our worst road trips ever. It was Chevy Chase movie material.

Busted in California

When we (and by *we* I mean *I*) bought the RV, I was making pretty good money working for a bank in Florida. My first big mistake was assuming I would have no problem finding a well-paying job right away when we landed back in California. After all, I was young, talented, and had a very impressive résumé.

What I didn't know was that the business market and economy in general were tanking in Southern California. In fact, it was one of those rare times in California when homes were actually depreciating. The housing bubble of the first decade of the new millennium had yet to implode.

During this time, thousands and thousands of people were being laid off. Businesses were downsizing like crazy.

I called everybody I knew. I was willing to drive hours one way to work if need be. I sent out more than fifty résumés and knocked on a bunch of doors. Nothing. No work anywhere. We went through our savings faster than a rat goes through a Cheeto. I ended up selling my guitar just to buy groceries for my babies.

You can imagine how excited I was to be making an RV payment every month. Laura's question, "And how are we going to pay for this?" haunted me.

I finally got a job completely outside of my field of experience, as a loan officer at a local bank. It was commission only and didn't offer any health benefits for ninety days. Why is it that you pay through the nose for health insurance all your life and never really need it until you don't have it?

One morning, my youngest son, Isaac, woke up, got out of bed, and collapsed with a scream of pain. He was five years old, and we had always thought he was pretty much indestructible. That kid had the highest pain tolerance of any boy I've ever seen. Sometimes, as a little tyke, he would fall hard, get up, shrug it off, and just keep on going without so much as a peep. When we heard him wailing from his bedroom, we knew it was something serious.

The doctor, whom we couldn't afford, sent us to the emergency room, which we couldn't afford. The ER doctor ran some tests, which we couldn't afford, and then admitted our son for more tests, which we couldn't afford. The diagnosis ended up being very serious. Isaac had a rare form of bone infection, which would require weeks of hospitalization, and which—you guessed it—we couldn't afford. I figured I was going to have to sell a kidney or something to pay for everything. I remember thinking, *God, what are you doing to me? I tithe faithfully. I serve you. I'm doing my best here. But I'm going bankrupt. What's up?*

I've discovered that asking God, "What's up?" is generally one of those questions he answers pretty clearly, especially when we need correction. As you may have noticed by now, I am exceptionally skilled at blame-shifting and denial. I do not like taking responsibility. I would rather blame God, or my dad, or my wife, or my dog, or somebody else—*anybody* else.

Here's the gist of what God taught me during that time of financial and emotional despair, another lesson learned the hard way: Providing for my every need is God's job; managing with wisdom what I have is mine.

Wall Street and Jesus

In Matthew 25, Jesus tells a parable about money management. Let me paraphrase what happened: The boss of a big and successful Wall Street investment firm is going away on a Caribbean cruise. He calls in three of his district managers and gives each one some financial responsibilities. One guy, probably the boss's son-in-law, gets a big chunk of change. Another guy gets a significant, though smaller, amount. The third guy, perhaps a new employee, gets relatively little. Each of these guys has been given something to manage and each has an equal opportunity to prosper. Jesus, the first equal opportunity employer.

Time passes, and the boss returns and calls his managers in for a financial report.

The kiss-up, overachieving son-in-law has done well. He doubled his investment. The second guy also doubled his assets. The newbie, however, turns out to be a slacker. He's got nothing to show for his work, though he managed not to lose the money he was given.

The boss gives a fantastic year-end bonus and stock options to the first two guys, but he fires the third guy.

What's the moral of this little story? Listen to what Jesus says: "Whoever has will be given more, and they will have an abundance. Whoever does not have, even what they have will be taken from them" (Matthew 25:29).

In other words, if you are faithful with what you have, and you manage it well, you will be entrusted with more. If you're not, you may lose it all. Faithfulness is a big deal to God. You see, everything we have belongs to him. He is the source of all our resources. He has promised to meet our needs. He will keep up his end of the deal, but we are responsible to manage well what he has given to us. Our bad decisions and lack of wisdom can't be blamed on God.

One of the Smartest Guys I Know

My stepdad, Frank Mayo, was one of the smartest and wisest money guys I've ever known. He recently went to be with the Lord, but for almost twenty-eight years he was a wonderful mentor to me. I was proud to call him Dad because he was a real father to me from the day he married my mom. Anything I now know about managing money, I learned from him. He used to say, "You've got to tell your money where to go or it just goes." Boy, did I learn that the hard way. It's another one of those life lessons I wish I had learned long before I reached adulthood.

That cursed RV ended up being repossessed. One of the most upsetting moments of my life came one Friday evening when a tow truck showed up at our house and I watched it drive off into the sunset with my RV.

I was completely maxed out on every credit card I had, to the tune of thousands of dollars. My son was miraculously healed after spending only a few days in the hospital, but those few days added up to a boatload of money. So on top of everything else, we now owed the hospital thousands of dollars as well.

Bottom line? I ended up filing for bankruptcy. I had failed miserably. I was embarrassed. My finances were a mess, and my pride was broken again over the condition we were in because of my foolish choices.

As Jesus said, "Whoever does not have, even what they have will be taken from them." You can drop in whatever terms you want—whoever does not have *wisdom, financial knowledge, economic diligence*—and the words are still so true.

Frank helped me put the pieces of my life back together. He taught me how to save. He taught me how to make a financial plan for the future. He helped me develop a simple budget and accounting mechanism that I still use to this day. He taught me how to tell my money where to go so it wouldn't just go.

As a pastor, I talk to people all the time who are in severe financial trouble. They are in it so deep they don't know which end is up. They want to give to God and his Kingdom's work through the church, but they're busted. We pastors can talk about tithing until Jesus comes back, and it's like talking to a first grader about calculus. Until some basic financial things are understood and practiced, many just won't have much to give to God.

At this writing, the average credit card debt per household in America is just under $16,000. That does not include what is owed for student loans, mortgages, and car loans. Approximately half of all credit card users pay only the minimum due each month. In other words, the typical American family is just one paycheck away from disaster.

So what do we do? How does grace work when we are so

far in the hole we can't see daylight? When discouraged by our financial failures, how does God's epic grace apply to our finances?

Let me give you a crash course in grace-based fiscal responsibility. It won't hurt, I promise.

First, you need to recognize and admit that it's time to get help. Most people have had little or no training in financial management. But it's out there. Find it. Start today and get whatever help you need. Our church offers a couple of financial courses on a regular basis. So do many others. (Check out www.daveramsey.com for some helpful resources.) You'll find that God's grace extends even into the financial realm of your life. Do not despair. Don't let shame or fear hold you back. Go for it.

Second, we—and I absolutely include myself in that *we*—need to redefine what we really need in this life. I'm afraid too many of us try to live above our means and above our true needs. We tend to trust in almighty plastic rather than in almighty God.

If you can't handle credit cards, cut them up. Get rid of them. Don't even keep one for emergencies. The next time something breaks down and you don't have the money in the bank to pay for it, pray. Cry out to God. Remember, he has promised to meet every legitimate need you have. You do your part, and he will absolutely do his.

Finally, ask God for help and wisdom. Besides learning to listen to my wife (thank God for her and the frugal Irish blood that flows within her), I'm learning to listen to God and to walk in his ways. God is pretty smart. It surprises me how much he knows about life and money. I have it on good authority and personal experience that God loves to come to our rescue with his safety net of epic grace.

Go ahead, decide now to go against the stream of our culture. Watch and see what happens as you trust in almighty God rather than in the not-so-almighty dollar.

Seriously, what's the worst that can happen?

11

LEARNING TO LOVE
A VDP

My command is this: Love each other as I have
loved you. Greater love has no one than this:
to lay down one's life for one's friends.

JOHN 15:12-13

MERCY IS *NOT* MY NATURAL GIFT, and patience with the weak
often eludes me. Add to that a dash of stubbornness mixed with
a pound of pride, and you've got a recipe for trouble. Over the
years, that combination of character weaknesses has made me
a prime target for what I call VDPs—*very draining persons.* A
more charitable person might call them EGRs—for *extra grace
required*—or maybe not even label them at all (imagine that).
But whatever you call them, the point is that they're not the
most comfortable kind of people to hang out with. And everybody has a VDP or two in their lives.

To the Least of These

The first VDP I encountered was a teenage girl named Patty.
I was a youth pastor at a large church, and she was one of the

kids in the youth group. She also happened to be mentally disabled. I know it sounds really terrible to call her a VDP. I know that a more mature and compassionate person would have loved her unconditionally. A godlier leader would have built her up and patiently endured her lack of social skills. I tried at first, but after a while (and I'm ashamed to admit this), Patty started to drive me crazy. Because everywhere I went during youth group or youth activities, Patty wasn't far behind.

Here's how our conversations always went . . .

"Hi, Kurt."

Sigh. "Hi, Patty."

"Whatcha doin', Kurt?"

"The same thing I was doing five minutes ago when you asked me for the twelfth time, Patty."

And then she would giggle, like it was all one big game.

That summer, at youth camp, we encouraged the kids to have a daily quiet time alone with God. Of course, that meant the staff also got some one-on-one time with Jesus. I was looking forward to an hour a day of peace and quiet—and no Patty.

On the second day of camp, with my Bible in one hand and my journal in the other, I set off into the woods for my quiet time. Finally, I was all alone for a much-needed encounter with God.

I found a great spot under a tall Douglas fir tree. The birds were in full chorus, the wind was blowing gently through the branches above, and the sun was shining—something we don't take for granted in Oregon. A tranquil brook flowed just to my right, and the sound of the water dancing over the rocks was a soothing balm. I was ready for an intimate and powerful time with God.

"Hi, Kurt. Whatcha doin'?"

"Patty! What are *you* doing? This is supposed to be our quiet time *alone* with God."

"Well . . . I don't like to be alone. Can I sit next to you today?"

I don't remember exactly what I said, but it was something rather harsh. I made it clear to Patty that it was not okay for her to sit next to me—not then; not ever—and I told her to go away. She didn't say a word. She just turned and slumped away. Rejected and wounded—by her pastor.

I know what you're thinking: *Bubna, you're a heartless idiot.*

Now that Patty was out of the way, I was ready for my spiritual time alone with God. Finally, an intimate and powerful time alone with my Maker. *Kumbaya, my Lord . . . Kumbaya . . .*

You can see where this is going.

As I started to pray, a wasp began buzzing around my head. I hate wasps. They must be a result of the Curse. Seconds later, as I was scrambling around trying to elude that persistent insect, a bird dropped a gooey bomb on my journal.

I screamed, "You've got to be kidding me!"

Then, while carefully attempting to clean off my journal with some water from the gently flowing creek, I dropped it. From *splat* to *splash* in thirty seconds.

I was *so* mad, I howled in disgust like a wounded bear. This was turning out to be the worst quiet time *ever*—and it was all Patty's fault, of course.

I finally got resettled and opened my Bible—and you will never guess what the reading was for that day. Matthew 25, the part where Jesus talks about loving and caring for "the least of these."

"I was hungry and you gave me something to eat, I was
thirsty and you gave me something to drink, I was a
stranger and you invited me in, I needed clothes and
you clothed me, I was sick and you looked after me,
I was in prison and you came to visit me."

Then the righteous will answer him, "Lord, when
did we see you hungry and feed you, or thirsty and
give you something to drink? When did we see you
a stranger and invite you in, or needing clothes and
clothe you? When did we see you sick or in prison
and go to visit you?"

The King will reply, "Truly I tell you, whatever you
did for one of the least of these brothers and sisters of
mine, you did for me." MATTHEW 25:35-40

Busted *again*. God has such a sense of humor. Even his grace
can be flavored with it at times. Of all the days to read this passage. As I read those words, I realized something, probably for
the first time. Jesus cares deeply about the disenfranchised, the
feeble, and the broken. In fact, how we love and treat the needy
directly affects him. "Whatever you do for the least of these . . .
you do for me."

Patty wasn't financially broken or in prison. She wasn't physically hungry or thirsty. But she was psychologically broken and
mentally in prison. She was emotionally hungry and thirsty for
unconditional love. Without a doubt, in the eyes of Jesus, she
qualified as "the least of these."

I started to weep. In that moment, I saw Patty from a vastly
different perspective.

God, how can I be so stupid? Why don't I see people the way you do? Why is my heart so cold?

I cried so hard and so long that the creek started to rise, or so it seemed. When I got done blubbering, I went to find Patty. She was sitting all by herself on a log near the softball field.

"Hi, Patty."

Now it was her turn to sigh with resignation. "Hi, Kurt . . ."

"Whatcha doin'?" I asked.

"Nothin'."

"Patty, I need to apologize and ask you to forgive me. What I said was unkind and not at all like Jesus. Will you forgive me?"

Instantly, and with a glow on her face, she said, "Yeah, it's okay. You're my best friend!"

And we were. From that day on, Patty and I were buds.

Over the next year or so, I learned more about unconditional love from my friendship with Patty than I have from any of my other friends. God used her to challenge me and change me in so many ways.

Why does God put people like Patty in our lives? To teach us how to love like he does. If we will let him, God uses difficult people to mold us into his image. They teach us patience. They teach us how to die to ourselves, how to lay down our lives for the sake of another. They teach us how to be more like Jesus. They stretch us into the far reaches of his epic grace.

I've never known a person with more joy than Patty.

I've never known a person as faithful and kind as Patty.

I've never been more unconditionally loved and accepted by anyone else in my entire life.

This mentally and socially challenged girl became one of my greatest teachers.

It wasn't easy. There were still lots of times when Patty pushed all my buttons. She soaked up my love and attention like a Texas desert, always wanting more, never seeming to get enough. I knew, however, that every time I hugged Patty, receiving a big bear hug in return from her, I was hugging Jesus, and he was hugging me.

Fast Forward to "Ta Jungle"

Years later, I started a new church in Tujunga, California, which we not-so-affectionately called Ta Jungle. Tujunga is probably best known as the town where a space alien landed in the movie *E.T.* (you can still see Elliott's house there today), and at the time I wouldn't have been surprised if a space alien *had* landed there. It was one of the weirdest places I've ever lived.

It was also a graveyard for churches. The ones that were there had always struggled, and new churches eventually died. Driving through town on Foothill Boulevard, you could just feel the ickiness everywhere. *But hey, let's start a new church here and see what happens!*

It was my first church start-up, and I was absolutely clueless. I'd had no formal or informal training on how to start a church. I didn't know what to do or what not to do. Laura and I had been attending The Church On The Way, which had a rather famous pastor named Jack Hayford. I figured I would just do what Jack does.

Big mistake.

For one thing, I was no Jack Hayford. I didn't have his experience, wisdom, or knowledge. I couldn't preach like he can and I didn't have his leadership skills. But I was never one to let ignorance stop me, so off we went into the abyss.

For some strange and still unknown reason, we actually started off pretty well. In no time, we had more than a hundred people attending our little storefront church in the middle of Tujunga. And what a group they were.

We had drug addicts and tattooed bikers. A transvestite named Cherrie, whose real name was Chuck. A former Canadian mobster (I didn't even know Canada had a mob) and an overly zealous and legalistic King-James-only Jesus freak named Phil. And those were the relatively normal people.

But you know what? I loved those people and I loved that church. I really did. We were like King David's band of misfits from 1 Samuel 22:2: "All those who were in distress or in debt or discontented gathered around him, and he became their leader." The distressed, the bankrupt, and the discontented. That was us—and it was glorious.

Guess who had prepared me to love people just like that? My friend Patty. More than thirty years have passed since I last saw Patty, but I've never forgotten her. She was a gift from God to me. Who in your life is that kind of gift?

Let's face it, people are weird sometimes. People can really snap our rubber bands and tweak our beaks. People can tick us off. But God uses people, even people we'd rather avoid, to mold us and make us more like him. It's not always pretty and it's seldom easy, but it's good to have a Patty or two in our lives. Whether these VDPs bring out the worst or the best in us is up to us.

Living in God's grace and extending it to others is a choice— and it's our calling.

12

WHAT THOSE ROMANCE NOVELS DON'T TELL YOU

Even though I walk through the darkest valley,

I will fear no evil, for you are with me.

PSALM 23:4

I WAS HAVING BREAKFAST ONE MORNING with my eldest son, Nathan, enjoying an exceptional cup of coffee and some scrumptious French toast. We were having a deep conversation about life and family and kids when he said, "Dad, do you know what my favorite biblical promise is?"

I responded with genuine curiosity, "Nope. Tell me."

"In this world you will have trouble." And he smiled.

The verse he referred to, John 16:33, contains some of the last words spoken by Jesus to his disciples just prior to his arrest and crucifixion: "I have told you these things, so that in me you may have peace. In this world you will have trouble. But take heart! I have overcome the world."

Jesus promises us trouble. Hmmmmm.

My first thought, of course, was about the loss of Nathan's son Phineas. That crisis was devastating for all of us. Then, in the next nanosecond or so, I thought about a bazillion other things Nathan has had to deal with in his life that definitely fall under the category of trouble. While my mind was rushing through his history, what struck me was the endearing Cheshire cat grin on his face. He truly is an amazing man.

Most of us would say the word *trouble* with disgust or despair, not with a smile. We *hate* trouble. We do everything and anything we can to avoid it. Trouble, for many, is a four-letter word.

But my remarkable son sat across the table from me with his Paul Newman steel-blue eyes as he quoted a favorite verse through an authentic smile the size of Texas, "In this world you will have trouble."

I love it when my kids teach me.

I love it when I can have a God-defining moment of revelation right in the middle of a mouth full of fat-saturated, syrup-smothered, butter-engulfed French toast.

I love it when I see something from a fresh and different perspective.

Jesus said in this life we would have trouble. Not just some of us, but all of us. Not just the foolish, but even the faithful. Not just the idiots who seem to deserve it, but the saints who don't (or so we think).

Life. Marriage. Family. Kids. They all share at least one thing in common: *trouble*.

Where did we get the idea it would be any other way?

When did we start to believe that we were guaranteed a trouble-free life?

What part of our existence on this crazy planet ever gave us the idea that life would be easy?

Seriously, who fed us this lie?

Yes, life is often good and better than we deserve. Life is frequently full of wonder more amazing than we can fathom with our tiny little brains. Granted, life is sometimes pretty epic. But life is hard, too, and repeatedly filled with challenges that can suck the marrow right out of our bones.

I'm not a pessimist. I'm really not one of those guys who sees only the dark side of everything and the glass half empty. As a general rule, I try to notice the beauty and good in this world.

The infectious giggle of a child.

The stunning glory of an exploding sunset over the ocean.

The miracle in the swift flight of a hummingbird or a playful swallow.

The majesty of a snow-covered mountain strutting its splendor through the clouds. (As I write this, Mount Hood is in view outside my hotel room window.)

I have so much to be thankful for, and I am surrounded by God's beauty revealed through so much of life. But life is still filled with trouble. It is an ever-present reality in this world. That's not pessimism; it's realism.

Marriage Trouble

Years ago, while I was a pastor in Portland, my wife and I went through a season of prolonged struggle in our marriage. We weren't on the verge of divorce. We just didn't like each other very much, and we were having a lot more conflict than fun. It wasn't the first time we'd been through a rough patch (and it wasn't the last time, either). But we needed some serious help.

I truly believe that marriage and trouble are almost synonymous. It's like Frick and Frack, Sonny and Cher, Sylvester and

Tweety, Simon and Garfunkel, Ben and Jerry, SpongeBob and Patrick . . . you really can't have one without the other. (Okay, maybe Simon did just fine on his own without Garfunkel, but it wasn't the same.)

Get married and you're pretty much guaranteed challenges, struggles, and trouble with a capital *T*! If you've been married for more than a week, you've probably already figured this out.

I've had hundreds of couples in my office, and I've heard one line more than I care to remember: "We're just not happy anymore. We think it's time to move on."

Are you *kidding* me? You're not happy anymore, and you think you can trade up for a newer, younger, hotter, better model of husband or wife, and that's where you'll find true happiness? That's just stupider than Jupiter.

But then I relax a bit, and I realize I have another opportunity to help a couple see what a counselor showed Laura and me years ago on a rainy day in Portland.

The counselor's name was Carol, and a friend had recommended her to us. We'd never been through any marriage counseling before, not even premarital counseling. Up until that point in my life, my attitude about counseling and counselors was fairly negative. "Only screwed up people who aren't smart enough to figure it out on their own need to pay somebody to help them."

Uhhhh . . . that would be me. We desperately needed help, and God sent Carol as a gift to us at just the right time in our marriage. (By the way, I now realize the wisdom in seeking out counseling whenever needed. Here's my best advice in six words: *Don't be stubborn. Get help now.*)

Carol did what good counselors do. She asked great questions and listened for the story behind the story. Often, the presenting issue is not the real issue, and rooting out the deeper truth is necessary.

Of course, I told her that Laura was the problem. I explained in graphic detail all of my wife's faults, and all my solutions to fix her many problems. Laura then had the gall to disagree with me. She told Carol—though in a much nicer way than I had spoken about her—a bunch of personal stuff about all *my* issues, and it embarrassed me.

What the heck, I thought, *this isn't why we're here! Get thee behind me, woman!*

Carol smiled and nodded her head in an annoying "I've seen this before" sort of way. Within moments, she turned our attention to something we both needed to hear, in a way that was about to rock our world.

Carol grabbed a piece of paper and a pen and drew a large circle on it. As she drew, she said, "This circle represents the covenant circle of love that God wants us to live in as married couples."

Covenant love in the Bible is the kind of love God has for us and the kind of love he wants us to experience with others. It is a commitment-based love built on a holy and mutual decision made by two people.

This is the kind of love Jeremiah writes about when he prophesies to Israel, "I have loved you with an everlasting love; I have drawn you with unfailing kindness" (Jeremiah 31:3).

It is what David declares when he writes in Psalm 103:17, "From everlasting to everlasting the LORD's love is with those who fear him."

Covenant love is not based on circumstances, feelings, or personal happiness. In fact, in a marriage, a covenant is a solemn accord between two people to love each other *no matter what.* It is the soul-binding vow spouses make to each other "to love and to cherish, in sickness and in health, for better or for worse, till death do us part." Covenant love in a marriage is not fickle or circumstantial; it is a lifelong agreement to cling to each other above all others and through all of life's many challenges.

As Carol drew her circle of covenant love, I could sense the presence of the Holy Spirit in the room saying, *Listen to this . . . it will change everything about everything in your marriage.*

At the top of the circle, Carol wrote the word *romance.*

She said, "This is the stage where every marriage relationship begins. It's fun. It's wonderful. It's exciting and electrifying. This is the season of your relationship, Laura, when you doodle his name; and it's the season, Kurt, when you can't get her out of your head."

I'm thinking, *Yeah, baby. Romance is hot! I love it. Sign me up for more.*

Then Carol burst my bubble with these painfully true words: "Romance is great, but romance is *not* a continual, never-ending state in any healthy marriage."

What? Why am I paying you for this? I'll take romance with a side of ranch dressing, thank you very much, and don't you dare tell me I can't have it!

The next word she wrote, just to the right of her stupid circle was the word *trouble.*

Without hesitation, and before I could cry foul, she said, "Trouble comes to every relationship. That's just the way it is."

That's it! I said to myself. *I'm outta here. This old gal is whacked. Trouble is normal? No stinkin' way!* Of course, I knew all relationships have trouble from time to time, but I never thought it was *normal*.

"Trouble," she went on to explain, "is that season of life when something unexpected and unwanted comes. Maybe it's something huge, like the loss of a job or a serious health issue. Maybe it's simply getting fed up with the husband for never putting down the toilet seat, or the wife for always leaving the cap off the toothpaste. Whatever the cause, trouble comes to all of us, and the romance fantasy usually gets destroyed."

Once I settled down a bit, it hit me. *Maybe she's on to something here. Maybe trouble is normal. Maybe I just need to accept it and move on.*

As I reflected on this insight, Carol wrote another word on her diagram, this time at the bottom of the circle in big, bold letters: *disillusionment*.

Almost in a whisper, she said, "This is the season when we must face our demons. It is the *valley of the shadow of death* in our relationships. Sadly, too many couples bail out here. In fact, about fifty percent of couples in our culture pull the plug on marriage during this season and fail to survive this difficult time."

In my mind, I ran through the hundreds of couples I knew who had done just that; they couldn't (or wouldn't) face the darkness in themselves or the darkness in their marriage. So they bailed, and many of them ran to another relationship in a tragic attempt to find romance with somebody else—looking for love in all the wrong places.

It started to dawn on me. *If romance is all we want, or all we will accept, then we are destined for tragedy in marriage. She's right; romance is great, but romance is not a continual, never-ending state in any healthy relationship.*

At that point in the counseling session, my brain was on overload. Frankly, I was more than just a little overwhelmed. I felt like a new father who'd just been told by the nurse that he was the proud father of quintuplets. "Wait, *what* did you say?"

In my ignorance and immaturity, I wanted blissful happiness and hot romance. I wanted a trouble-free marriage that was easy and always fun. But now I realized that what I wanted doesn't exist. Not in the real world.

Trouble is normal.

Disillusionment is a dark valley through which we all must navigate.

Where did we get the idea that marriage would *ever* be easy?

I was shocked back to consciousness as Carol wrote another word—this time on the left side of the circle. It was the word *joy*.

With a knowing smile on her face, she said, "Joy is the next season you will experience if you remain faithful and true during the valley of disillusionment. Joy is far more than happiness. Joy is that deep satisfaction and delight you have when you realize the depth of your commitment to love each other no matter what."

I looked over at my wife, and she was crying. I started to cry. Carol started to cry. Good grief. We passed the Kleenex box, and then we all took a deep breath of relief.

As Carol handed us that simple sheet with what I now believed to be the most powerful drawing I'd ever seen, she said, "Here's the last thing you need to know: I've drawn this as a circle because the seasons will come and go. Joy always leads to another season of romance . . . which always leads to another season of trouble . . . which always leads to disillusionment . . . which always leads to more joy—*if* you hang in there."

Over the years, I've shared this same picture with literally thousands of other couples. I've taught the four stages in churches. I've drawn it on napkins at Starbucks for young starstruck couples. I've given to many others the gift of God's epic grace that Carol gave to Laura and me on that rainy day in Portland so long ago. And it really is a gift of God's grace when you understand his truth and are bathed in his hope.

Whatever trouble has soiled your marriage and dragged you kicking and screaming into the valley of the shadow of death, hold on. Remember, trouble is not the end of the story. As Jesus also says in John 16:33, "Take heart! I have overcome the world."

I understand there are thousands of *what ifs* and times when one of the marriage partners gives up, and it breaks our hearts.

But by God's grace, and in his strength, *you* must choose to stay true.

Remain faithful.

Don't give up on God or on your spouse.

I know from personal experience that God does some of his best work in the midst of some very dark and empty places, and that joy is just around the corner.

13
LOST!

*Let us not neglect our meeting together, as some people do,
but encourage one another, especially now that
the day of his return is drawing near.*

HEBREWS 10:25, NLT

MY SENSE OF DIRECTION IS SENSELESS. In fact, I'm very directionally challenged. I can't tell you which way is west unless I see the sun setting, and even then I might have a problem. I'm lost, clueless, and confused on a regular basis. Scary. Sad. But so true.

When my son Nathan was in high school, he and I and some friends successfully climbed to the summit of Mount Hood in Oregon. As mountain climbs go, Mount Hood is challenging, but not so demanding or technical that it requires special training. It's pretty much a long, windy climb up a steep, snowy mountain, following a well-worn trail to the top. It's hard to get lost on a goat trail.

Watching the sun rise from the 11,000-foot summit was an awesome experience. (I think it rose in the east.) I treasure the memory of that adventure with my son.

Two years later, a different group of friends and I decided it was time to tackle Washington's Mount Adams. Again, it was not a technically challenging climb, just another long hike in the snow.

On the Mount Hood climb, I used my own boots and rented crampons. (A crampon is a spiked steel framework that attaches to the bottom of a boot to prevent slipping when climbing on ice and snow.) The crampons kept coming off my boots, which made the climb a bit more difficult and frustrating. So for Adams, I decided to rent climbing boots with a set of crampons specially made for the boots. What a big mistake.

Wearing rented boots is like chewing with somebody else's dentures. They don't quite fit and they hurt like heck. Because the boots were broken in by somebody else's feet, the contours and nuances of my feet didn't match the shape of the boots. As you can imagine, this resulted in hot spots, which led to blisters. Big blisters.

Halfway through the climb, my feet were killing me. Every step was painful. I wasn't thinking about the cold. I wasn't worrying about the wind. I wasn't concerned with the steepness of the climb. All I could think about—every step along the way—was, *Bubna, you're an idiot for renting these boots. Who rents boots for a hike, let alone a mountain climb!*

After climbing for about seven hours, we stopped for a rest and some water. I had some dry socks in my pack, and the socks I had on felt very wet, so I decided to put the dry ones on. As I took off my boots, I realized why they felt so wet. My feet were *bleeding.* On each of my heels was a bleeding crater about the size of a fifty-cent piece, and those were just the big ones. My feet were an ugly mess, and I knew I was in trouble. We still had at least an hour of climbing ahead of us, and then several hours of hiking back down. At that point, I made another idiotic decision. I decided to turn back and head down the mountain by myself.

Rule number one of mountain climbing is to have the right gear, which of course includes good boots. Rule number two is to never climb alone; stay with your group. I knew this. I knew better. Going off by myself was dumb. If you can't continue with your group, you hunker down and stay put until they return for you. You don't go wandering off alone. *Ever*. Nevertheless, off I went, assuming I would just retrace my steps and end up where we had started. Have I mentioned that I'm directionally challenged and get lost easily?

Dumb and Dumber

On the way down, following the well-worn trail, I came to a place where some Boy Scouts were camping. Rather than climb the mountain all at once, the Scouts went halfway the first day, camped at a clearing for the night, and then summited the next day. When I reached their camp on the way down, I came to a split in the trail. I could either go right or left. I could have sworn that I needed to go right, but right was wrong. In choosing the trail to the right, I made another critical error, but it took me about an hour to realize I was lost. No trail to follow. No signs. Nobody else around. No compass. No clue.

At first, I was mad. How could I be so stupid? Then I thought about going back the way I had come. The smart thing at that point would have been to retrace my steps back to the Boy Scout camp, but every step was excruciating.

Besides my bloody feet, I was now out of water and out of

food. I was tired and not thinking clearly. (Boy, is that an under-statement.) So I continued to press on. I figured that as long as I was headed downhill, when I got to the bottom I could go to the left along flat ground until I found the trailhead where we had started.

If you've ever wondered how someone could get so far off course in life, I have a simple answer. One dim-witted mistake after another.

Another hour or so passed and I still had no idea where I was. Now I was starting to panic. When you're all alone, cold, tired, dehydrated, and miserable, you start to imagine dying on the back side of the mountain and not being found until spring when the snow melts. I knew I was in hot water on a cold mountain all by myself and that things were about to go from bad to really bad.

I came to a clearing below a ridge that ran along the top of a large bowl. The smart thing to do would have been to climb up the ridge about thirty yards or so and traverse along the top. But because I was extremely tired and in pain, going up was not an option for me. Instead, I decided to traverse across and down the bowl, just below the ridge, in an attempt to get to the other side as easily as possible.

I was about halfway across the bowl when the snow beneath my feet began to move. Before I could even stop to think, I was moving right along with it. I had started an avalanche!

What little mountain training I'd had had taught me what to do in the event of an avalanche. The most important thing is not to get buried. Don't worry about your gear or anything else. Try to swim with it and stay on top, because people who get buried under tons of snow tend to die.

It all happened so fast and was so surreal that it's hard to describe what I did or how I felt. Suddenly, I wasn't thinking about how tired I was or how horribly my feet hurt. All I remember thinking was, *God, it's the day before Father's Day. This would be a lousy day to die!* I let go of everything and did my best to surf the wave of snow that was carrying me down the mountain.

When I stopped, I was facing uphill and buried up to my chest. Above me, all the way up the bowl for a hundred yards or so, I could see pieces of my gear littering the hillside. A glove, my backpack, my hat, and one of my walking poles marked the line of my descent.

My hands were free and my arms weren't broken, so I immediately started digging my way out of the snow. It's amazing what you can do when you're terrified and pumped full of adrenaline.

I will never forget how I felt when I got free of that snow. For one thing, I couldn't stop shaking. My whole body was trembling. Emotionally, I knew I'd just dodged a bullet. Near-death experiences can leave you a bit euphoric. I just kept saying over and over again, "Thank you, God. Thank you! Thank you! Thank you! You rescued me again."

Inching my way back up the hillside, I gathered some of my missing gear—like my backpack with the first aid kit in it—and slapped a large Band-Aid on a cut on my leg. Then I sat for a moment, gathering my wits and wondering if I had survived the avalanche only to face death from exposure.

My euphoria was quickly dissolving into deep concern.

It was so quiet.

I felt so alone.

I hadn't seen or heard anyone for several hours. I didn't know how I was going to get up and keep going. My thanks to God now turned into a desperate cry for help.

"Father, I'm so sorry for being so stupid . . . please don't let me die out here."

At that very moment—I kid you not—I heard laughter.

"That's not funny, God," I said out loud. "Laughing at me is not going to help."

Then I realized it was a couple of guys who were hooting and hollering and having a grand old time. I found out later they had spent the night camping not far from where I was and were throwing snowballs at each other and just having fun.

When I realized there were living, breathing human beings within earshot of where I sat, I started to yell for help at the top of my lungs. Trust me, when you're desperate, looking cool means absolutely nothing. Being self-sufficient and manly means zip. I yelled like a baby, and I didn't care what anybody thought. I just wanted to be rescued.

Within moments, I saw a guy standing on a hill about two or three hundred yards away. He waved.

I yelled, "Help! I need help!"

When I reached the top of the hill, the two guys gave me some food and water and then escorted me to the main trail—which was in the opposite direction from where I had been headed.

Eventually, by God's grace, I found my friends at the trailhead and survived another day of stupidity. That was also my last attempt at mountain climbing. As a Father's Day gift to my wife, I promised to leave mountain climbing to the professionals.

The Problem with Isolation

I learned a lot through that experience.

I learned *not* to rent boots.

I learned not to take what appears to be the easy way.

Most important, I learned how foolish it is to get isolated. We need each other. We weren't made to be alone.

The first time the word *alone* is used in the Bible is in Genesis 2:18, when God, after creating Adam, says, "It is not good for the man to be alone."

In Numbers 11:16-17, God tells Moses to gather seventy of Israel's elders and leaders to help him manage the people, saying, "They will share the burden of the people with you so that you will not have to carry it alone."

Even Jesus told his disciples, "I am not alone, for my Father is with me" (John 16:32).

We weren't made to live life on our own. It's not healthy for us to be alone. When we get isolated, we get into trouble.

I know this flies in the face of the rugged individualism that is prized in American culture—the macho, I-don't-need-nobody mind-set. I understand why we sometimes think that alone is better, because people only let us down. I recognize how hard it can be to lean on someone for support, only to have them hurt you more than they help. I know how heartbreaking it is to be connected to somebody and to share the deepest part of who you are, and to wind up having them shred your soul to pieces.

But I know that when we get isolated, even worse things can happen. It's too easy to get blindsided or to do something stupid. We need the wisdom and counsel of others who love us and have our best interests in mind.

The wisest guy to ever live, a king named Solomon, once wrote these words of advice:

As iron sharpens iron, so a friend sharpens a friend.
PROVERBS 27:17, NLT

The way of fools seems right to them, but the wise
listen to advice.
PROVERBS 12:15

Listen to advice and accept discipline, and at the end
you will be counted among the wise.
PROVERBS 19:20

I think you see his point. Left to ourselves, we can become
relationally and spiritually dull and often end up taking a very
foolish path. Of course, the key component here is *heeding* the
advice and wisdom of others. My mountain-climbing friends
tried to tell me not to go off by myself. I blew them off and
ended up getting blown off the mountain. "The way of fools
seems right to them, but the wise listen."

Herbert the Hermit

Tragically, I could tell you a hundred stories of people who
chose not to listen and who decided to go it alone.

Let me tell you about Herbert (not his real name). Herbert is
brilliant. On the IQ scale, he's way up there in the genius range.
He graduated from one of the best schools in the country. He's
got not one but two master's degrees. He's also self-taught in the
languages of the Bible (Greek and Hebrew) and has an impressive knowledge of church history.

I like Herb. He's fun to debate and always adds lots of

seasoning to any discussion, spiritual or otherwise. But somewhere along on his journey, Herb stopped listening. He got lost in his books and his computer stuff and decided he really didn't need other people. Not his friends, not his family, and certainly not a middle-IQ, plain old pastor like me.

It didn't happen overnight, but before long, Herb started to drift further and further away. Church became a waste of time. He became cynical and critical. In the few conversations he had with real, living, breathing people, he oozed disdain, and the more he drifted, the more isolated he became.

Last I heard, he was divorced and working out of his home, alone, in Los Angeles—by all definitions, a hermit. What a loss for the Kingdom of God.

When we get isolated, we get into trouble. I know Herb's story is a bit extreme and unusual (at least I hope it is), but his problem is not that rare. Too many people think they can stand on their own two feet, and too many believe they can make it on their own.

In nearly thirty years of pastoring, I've seen hundreds of people isolate and insulate themselves from the very people that God put in their lives to help them. They chose to wander off on their own (sometimes taking their spouse and kids with them, but isolated nonetheless), and they ended up far from the path God wanted for them. It breaks my heart. I know it breaks the heart of God. He didn't make us to be alone. He created us to function within a family of origin and a family of faith.

From time to time I hear Christians say, "I don't need the church. I've got Jesus, and that's good enough." They grumble about hypocrisy in the church. They are intolerant of organizational ineptitudes. They can't stand "two-faced" leaders, who say one thing and do another.

I've heard these complaints, and many more, and I never argue with them. Frankly, they're often right. As an organization, the church is an imperfect entity with plenty of hypocrisy and duplicity. In many ways, we have a long and inglorious history that is nothing to brag about. I get it. I know.

However, what these people seem not to understand is that the church, with all its warts and wrinkles, is still the body of Christ. In fact, we are the bride of Christ, and as such, we are—and always will be—unbelievably precious to Jesus.

My wife is not perfect, but she's still my wife. My love for her and my ongoing relationship with her are not based on her performance. Because of who she is, I am to love her unconditionally. Likewise, because of who the church is, not just what people do or don't do, we are to love her as Jesus does.

We *need* the church. It is God's instrument for reaching the world.

We need *each other*. We are God's instrument for building up one another, and we are told to "motivate one another to acts of love and good works" (Hebrews 10:24, NLT).

Sometimes when we're in pain, hurting and bleeding like I was on Mount Adams, we walk away from the very people we need to stay connected with. In fact, oftentimes the necessary antidote to our pain is found in the relationships we have with others. It might seem easier and better to go it alone, but we weren't made to fly solo.

A friend of mine often says, "We were made out of community *for* community." That is, out of the ultimate and perfect community of God the Father, God the Son, and God the

Holy Spirit, we were formed to live and breathe within a far less perfect community of vital relationships within the body of Christ—the church.

God help us, we need one another.

We can fight that reality, or we can embrace it.

14

WILD HOGS

A friend loves at all times, and a brother
is born for a time of adversity.

PROVERBS 17:17

LET ME EXPAND ON WHAT I TALKED ABOUT in the last chapter by specifically addressing the issue of friendship.

A movie came out in 2007 called *Wild Hogs*, starring Tim Allen, John Travolta, Martin Lawrence, and William H. Macy. It was a bit crude and crass at times, but funny nonetheless. The plot was simple: Four guys go through a midlife crisis and they all have motorcycles (the best midlife therapy there is, by the way). They end up going on a road trip filled with trouble and conflict, but it is their friendship that sustains them and carries them through one struggle after another.

Here's what struck me as I watched this flick: Life was meant to be experienced with close friends. We need friends. We need others. We need people in our lives we can count on through thick and thin. In fact, let me say it again: God *never* meant for us to be alone.

Alone we get deceived.

Alone we get devoured.

Alone we get self-focused, rather than others-focused.

Alone we get overpowered and defeated.

That is why God never meant for us to be alone. Here is the wisdom of Solomon on the matter:

Two people are better off than one, for they can help each other succeed. If one person falls, the other can reach out and help. But someone who falls alone is in real trouble. Likewise, two people lying close together can keep each other warm. But how can one be warm alone? A person standing alone can be attacked and defeated, but two can stand back-to-back and conquer. Three are even better, for a triple-braided cord is not easily broken. ECCLESIASTES 4:9-12, NLT

Most of us understand this wisdom. We see the common sense in it and recognize the dangers of becoming isolated. However, sometimes we still isolate and insulate rather than integrate our lives into the mix with others. Sometimes, when we're hurt or angry, we cower in a dark corner like a wounded, whimpering dog.

The Battle Rages

Recently, my life has been complicated more than usual by a series of events that are pretty much out of my control . . .

- I blew my back out a couple of months ago. Now every day I ache and most nights I sleep poorly. Add to this that I suffer from calcific tendinitis in my shoulder and have the knees of a ninety-year-old.

- My dear wife is going through some pretty tough physical challenges of her own as she wrestles with type 2 diabetes.
- At the church I pastor, we're in the midst of a building campaign in which we need to raise about three-quarters of a million dollars. I know God has led us to this endeavor, but in the shadow of what has been called the Great Recession, my faith is certainly being tested.

All of these things tend to make me want to crawl under a nice warm blanket in a fetal position and isolate myself from the big, bad world. My natural inclination is to withdraw to the safety of my own little world; but that's not the wise thing to do.

So instead of retreating into isolation, I force myself to engage. I push myself to connect. I find ways to better bind myself to others, because I know and believe what it says in Ecclesiastes 4:12: "A cord of three strands is not quickly broken."

Life in a Hole

I have a buddy I've known for a very long time. I would do anything I could for him. I value his friendship and thank God for his life. He's an extremely gifted and talented man who has been powerfully used by God in many amazing ways.

However, he has one nasty habit: When his life gets hard, he pretty much drops off the planet. He buries himself in a hole so deep you can't even find him, let alone help him. He doesn't respond to e-mails. He doesn't return calls. And if you do track him down, he makes it painfully clear: "Go away and leave me alone."

I understand his pain and empathize with his struggles. I've been there, too, but I also know how foolish it is to drop out and run.

When I get alone with just me, myself, and I, the only voices I tend to hear are the enemy's and my own all-too-often-not-so-healthy self-talk. I start to believe the lies of Satan, and I typically talk myself into a deeper hole of despair.

Many years ago, while pastoring a small church in Portland, I went through a terrible season of serious doubt. It was like a heavy, wet blanket was smothering my soul.

I doubted my call.

Am I really supposed to do this?

I doubted my abilities.

Can I do this?

I doubted the people in our little church.

Do they even like me?

And eventually, I doubted God.

Why did you bring me here? Do you hate me, God?

There were a few friends I should have talked to and shared my struggles with, but I was too proud to be that transparent. Once again, I was an idiot. And I ignored the experience of grace through others that was just a phone call, e-mail, or conversation away from me.

My amazing wife was with me every step along the way, but I hid the depths of my despair from her because I didn't want to burden her. Turns out she knew what I was going through (nothing is ever really hidden).

Why do we tend to withdraw? Why do we isolate ourselves?

Why do we think we can either get through it on our own or fear what others will think of us if they see our struggles?

Right now, about seven billion people inhabit planet Earth. That's a lot of people, and plenty of folks are available to help us up when we fall. But instead of reaching out for help, we tend to build walls between ourselves and the very ones we need.

One day, in the middle of my crisis of confidence, my good friend Kip Jacob called me up and said, "Hey, do you have time for lunch?"

I wanted to say, "No. Just leave me alone."

Somehow, though, I knew God was reaching out to me through this trusted friend to pull me out of the hole I had fallen into. Two days later, over a burger and some fries, Kip helped me to my feet again, and I'm pretty sure he saved me from chucking it all and walking away from ministry for good.

It really is true—two are better than one.

My current struggles are hard, but I'm not in despair or doubt because I've learned to take full advantage, in a positive way, of the wonderful relationship I have with my wife and the friendship of several men who consistently support me through life's challenges.

I know I'm not alone.

I can't imagine my life without their love and support.

When life gets hard, I know it might seem easier to go it alone. I understand how tempting it is to withdraw into a pity party of misery, anguish, and hopelessness.

I've heard people say as they isolate and hide themselves, "I just need to get alone with God."

Trust me, I understand the wisdom and value of one-on-one times with just God. But God made us to be in fellowship with others as well. He wired us to find comfort, consolation, and wisdom in the context of friendship. He designed us to need one another. Life was never meant to be a journey alone.

Rugged individualism might be a valued character trait in our culture, but in the Kingdom of God we are to be *interdependent*, not independent.

We all need a great friend who will stick closer to us than a brother (or sister). We need someone, or a small group of someones, with whom we can be honest and to whom we can reveal our deepest and darkest struggles. We need someone who will love us in our worst moments. We need a friend who can handle the nakedness of our souls and not freak out.

If you don't have that kind of friend, ask God for one. He has promised to meet our every need, including our need for deep friendship.

If you do have a bosom buddy, nurture and cherish that relationship for all it is worth. That relationship is a priceless gift from God.

So the next time you find yourself starting to feel overcome by life, don't hesitate for a second to grab the phone and call someone for help. And if a friend calls you, be sure not to push him or her away.

That's what friends are for.

It's the way God meant for it to be.

Seriously, you are not strong enough, smart enough, or even mentally sound enough to handle everything life will throw at you. But that's okay. That's why we need other people.

15

LESSONS I LEARNED ON A SCOOTER

Trust in the LORD with all your heart and lean not

on your own understanding; in all your ways submit

to him, and he will make your paths straight.

PROVERBS 3:5-6

A VERY LONG TIME AGO, I was the not-so-proud owner of a Yamaha 50 scooter. Nowadays, I drive a Vulcan 1500 Classic, which is way cooler. But back then, that little scooter was all I could afford and the best I could do for cheap transportation.

In 1988, we moved to the town of Vista, in northern San Diego County, to help with a new start-up church. The church was actually located in Oceanside, but we chose to live in Vista, the community right next door, because we were told it had better schools.

The church grew very rapidly, and after about six months, the senior pastor asked me to join the staff as his assistant. I was thrilled to be given the opportunity. But because it was a new and young church, finances were tight, and I took a huge cut in pay to go on staff. But Laura and I felt it was worth it, and we were willing to make the necessary sacrifices.

At that time, we had only one car and couldn't afford to buy another one for me to drive to work. The church office was only about ten miles from our home, but with four kids and a busy schedule of her own, Laura couldn't get by without a car, and it was very inconvenient for her to take me to work and pick me up every day. So I decided to look for something inexpensive and easy to maintain that would get me to and from the church.

I'm a guy who drove muscle cars in his teens and early twenties. They were big, fast, and cool cars like Trans Ams and Mustangs. Once upon a time, I drove a very speedy Honda 750 to work on the California highways every day. So you can understand how driving a scooter that had a top speed of about 35 mph going downhill was embarrassing. I usually couldn't even drive in the normal traffic lanes. I had to stay in the bike lane—and at times, even the bikes would pass me.

I did this for more than a year, and for a long time I truly hated that little scooter. Every ride on that tiny, wimpy, ridiculous excuse for a motorbike threatened my ego and my manhood.

I know, I'm an idiot.

During that year, however, God began to teach me another valuable life lesson through my long, slow, embarrassing drives to work. Here's what I learned on that crazy scooter: God will use whatever means necessary to create in us the likeness and character of his Son. He is absolutely committed to our spiritual growth. In fact, God is far more concerned with our growth than he is with our comfort.

I wish I could tell you that God is all about making our lives easy and fun. But sometimes God will allow our lives to be hard enough for us to learn what he wants us to know. Sometimes the only way to develop us is to test us. Sometimes he will squeeze us, trim us, and mold us until we actually hurt.

I faced many tests of my character on that little scooter.

One day, it was rather cold for California and very windy, so I was all bundled up in a coat, warm gloves, and my Snoopy scarf. I was about halfway to the office and crawling along at a top speed of about 32 mph. There was one section of road that was four lanes wide and the speed limit was 45 mph, but most of the people were buzzing by me at fifty-five or better. I was driving in the bike lane, just trying to stay out of the way and stay alive.

All of a sudden, a car flew by me with its horn honking. I just about fell off my scooter in terror. I wasn't sure what the driver's problem was, and I thought about saluting him with one particular finger. I didn't, but he turned around anyway, and then went flying by me again—horn blaring—in the opposite direction. This time, I noticed it was a car full of high school boys, and they were all laughing at me.

I knew trouble was afoot. There was no place to hide and no way I was going to outrun them. Sure enough, I looked back in time to see them turning around to make another pass at me.

I started to pray, "O God, O God, O God! Please transport me immediately to my destination, like you did with Philip in Acts 8. Otherwise, this is gonna be bad."

And it was. On their final pass, one of the boys took the opportunity to toss a Mega Gulp cup of cola onto my back. Of course, they thought it was hilarious, but I drove the next five miles to the office wet, cold, sticky, and ticked off.

I didn't blame God for what happened (though it would have

been nice to have been teleported), but he always uses the trials and tests of life to mold and shape us into the image of his Son.

Three Tests

Years ago, Ron Mehl, a great pastor and teacher from Beaverton, Oregon, who has since gone to be with the Lord, taught me about three great tests that God tends to put us all through. I'm borrowing from his insights here.

In the book of Genesis, chapters 12 through 15, we find the story of a guy named Abraham. He's also mentioned in Paul's letter to the Romans (chapter 4) and in the book of Hebrews, which is where we find a summary of the three tests God put him through.

> By faith Abraham, when called to go to a place he would later receive as his inheritance, obeyed and went, even though he did not know where he was going. By faith he made his home in the promised land like a stranger in a foreign country; he lived in tents, as did Isaac and Jacob, who were heirs with him of the same promise. For he was looking forward to the city with foundations, whose architect and builder is God.
>
> By faith Abraham, even though he was past age—and Sarah herself was barren—was enabled to become a father because he considered him faithful who had made the promise. And so from this one man, and he as good as dead, came descendants as numerous as the stars in the sky and as countless as the sand on the seashore. . . .

By faith Abraham, when God tested him, offered Isaac as a sacrifice. He who had received the promises was about to sacrifice his one and only son, even though God had said to him, "It is through Isaac that your offspring will be reckoned." Abraham reasoned that God could raise the dead, and figuratively speaking, he did receive Isaac back from death.

HEBREWS 11:8-12, 17-19

This is an amazing passage of Scripture that summarizes the life and faith of Abraham. Let's see what we can learn from his journey.

The Test of the Unknown

Look again at the opening statement in the passage from Hebrews 11: "By faith Abraham, when called to go to a place he would later receive as his inheritance, obeyed and went, even though he did not know where he was going." We can call this first test the test of the *unknown*.

God called Abraham away from his homeland and his family to an unfamiliar place. God didn't give him any details. He didn't provide a trip itinerary or a tour guide. He simply said, "Go into the unknown and trust that I will lead you" (my paraphrase).

The test of the unknown is really a test of *direction*. Who is going to lead us? Who are we going to obey? Who are we going to follow?

The test of the unknown is intentionally designed by God to reveal our confidence in him. I can *say* that I trust God. I can *say* that I will follow him wherever he leads. I can *say* that he's in charge of my life. But when it comes right down to it, will

I follow and trust in him, even when I don't know where I'm going and even when I don't understand? Will I do what God asks me to do and step into the unknown by faith?

For me, leaving the security of a well-paying and secure job in banking to take that job in Oceanside, at a new church and in a new town, was a test of the unknown. I thought about it a lot on those scooter rides to the office.

Will I entrust my life and my livelihood to God?

Will I live my life for him, or am I just going to live it for myself and what I want?

The test of the unknown—this test of direction—is important because it forces us to make a decision regarding our faith in God.

The Test of the Unfulfilled

In Genesis 12:2, God tells Abraham, "I will make you into a great nation." The promise to Abraham was clear. It was the promise of many descendants.

Abraham first received this promise when he was seventy-five years old, but it wasn't until he was one hundred—twenty-five years later!—that he finally had a son through his wife, Sarah. It wasn't just a year or five years or even ten years. They waited a quarter of a century to see just the beginning of the fulfillment of this promise from God. We can call this second test the test of the *unfulfilled*.

I really don't enjoy waiting. I'm not very patient. A while back, I ordered a book online and somehow they mailed it to the wrong person somewhere in Connecticut. The book was out of print and from a used book dealer, and it took almost two months to finally get it in my hands. It was very frustrating, even though it was just a book. Imagine waiting twenty-five years for the promise of a son.

Waiting can be hard.

This test of the unfulfilled is extremely challenging for most of us. But the test of the unfulfilled is really a test of *dependence*. When the promise of God comes slowly, who are we going to depend on?

When things don't happen fast enough for our liking, and when it may even seem as if the promise will never be fulfilled, what will we do?

Will we take matters into our own hands?

Will we give up in despair?

Will we throw up our hands in frustration and anger?

Or will we trust that God is faithful and true to his word? Listen to what the apostle Paul writes about Abraham:

When God promised Abraham that he would become the father of many nations, Abraham believed him. God had also said, "Your descendants will be as numerous as the stars," even though such a promise seemed utterly impossible! And Abraham's faith did not weaken, even though he knew that he was too old to be a father at the age of one hundred and that Sarah, his wife, had never been able to have children.

Abraham never wavered in believing God's promise. In fact, his faith grew stronger, and in this he brought glory to God. He was absolutely convinced that God was able to do anything he promised.

ROMANS 4:18-21, NLT

Frankly, there have been times in my life when I've been *anything but* "absolutely convinced that God was able to do anything he promised."

There have been times when I've taken matters into my own hands in a vain and idiotic attempt to force God's hand. However, when I have waited on him, and when I have depended on him even when he seems slow, the end result has always been good. God doesn't lie. He doesn't forget his promises, and his timing is always perfect.

Abraham "made his home in the promised land like a stranger in a foreign country" (Hebrews 11:9), and even though Sarah was barren, "he considered him faithful who had made the promise" (Hebrews 11:11).

Abraham believed that God was faithful to his word.

The Test of the Unforeseen

Let's look again at Hebrews 11:17-18: "By faith Abraham, when God tested him, offered Isaac as a sacrifice. He who had received the promises was about to sacrifice his one and only son, even though God had said to him, 'It is through Isaac that your offspring will be reckoned.'"

Imagine how confused and perplexed you would be if, after you've waited for twenty-five years to receive the promise, God comes and wants to take it away from you. That is exactly what happened to Abraham in Genesis 22. He is told by God to take Isaac to a mountain in the region of Moriah and sacrifice him there as a burnt offering. I'm sure that Abraham did not see that coming. That's why we call this third and final test the test of the *unforeseen*.

To our way of thinking, and from our human perspective,

God's command doesn't make any sense. What possible good could come from sacrificing Isaac? That's insane, right?

I don't know about you, but besides being impatient, I can be rather possessive. Once I get what I want, you're going to have to pry it from my cold, dead fingers to get it away from me. That's why it's hard for me to relate to Abraham's faith in God here. But this test of the unforeseen is really a test of *devotion*.

The real question is what or who are we going to love the most? Will it be the promise or the Promised One? By the way, God doesn't test us because he's insecure. It's not because he's sadistic and gets some warped pleasure out of giving and then taking away. He tests us because he knows that when we love *him* first, everything else comes into focus.

God is not trying to cheat us or rip us off. He wants to *bless* us. By testing us with unforeseen circumstances, he teaches us firsthand what it means to live by faith through grace. He shows us what it means to genuinely trust in him, and how to experience his grace and goodness even when we don't understand everything that happens in our lives. Whatever he gives us can only truly be a blessing when we hold it loosely and when God is first and foremost in our lives.

During my scooter-riding days, Laura and I were pretty poor. Many times while I was putt-putting along in the bike lane, I thought, *God, when are you going to bless us with enough money to buy a real vehicle?*

Just about every time I got on that silly scooter, I thought about money and my lack of it. Until one day it hit me: "I'm more devoted to getting more money than I am to getting more of God in my heart and life."

Believe me when I say that if you love something or someone

more than you love God, he *will* test and challenge you in that area with unforeseen circumstances that usually stretch you way beyond yourself. God tests us because he really does have our best interests in mind.

Here is what Moses told the children of Israel: "The LORD your God is testing you to find out whether you love him with all your heart and with all your soul. It is the LORD your God you must follow, and him you must revere. Keep his commands and obey him; serve him and hold fast to him" (Deuteronomy 13:3-4).

If you're at all like me, you don't like the test of the unforeseen and the test of devotion, but this is what God does to reveal whether we love him with all our heart and soul. By trusting and obeying God, Abraham demonstrated his heart for the Lord. He showed that no one and nothing meant more to him than God. Here's how this story ends:

> Abraham took the knife and lifted it up to plunge it into his son, to slay him.
>
> At that moment the Angel of God shouted to him from heaven, "Abraham! Abraham!"
>
> "Yes, Lord!" he answered.
>
> "Lay down the knife; don't hurt the lad in any way," the Angel said, "for I know that God is first in your life—you have not withheld even your beloved son from me." GENESIS 22:10-12, TLB

When you drive a scooter, you learn to expect the unexpected. Potholes, swerving cars, vicious demonized dogs that come out of nowhere and can run faster than you can possibly go.

Anything can happen. You learn that life can and will throw you a curveball from time to time. And it usually happens when you least expect it and at the very worst possible time.

When life surprises you—and it will—what are you going to do?

Who will you trust?

Where will you turn for help?

Who will you love the most?

Remember this: God will use whatever means necessary to bring ongoing spiritual development into our lives. He really is far more concerned with our growth than he is with our comfort.

His goal is not our misery; it is our molding. It is to see us transformed into the image of Jesus Christ in our character, in our minds, and in our hearts.

I eventually gave that scooter away to someone who needed it more than I did. And by then I had a car. I wonder what lessons the next owner learned on that silly scooter.

I wonder what lessons God has in store for *you*. I suspect they will have little to do with the vehicle you use. They'll likely have far more to do with the grace-paved road you choose to travel and the attitude you have while you are cruising along.

16

CALEB

That is what the Scriptures mean when they say,
"No eye has seen, no ear has heard, and no mind has
imagined what God has prepared for those who love him."

1 CORINTHIANS 2:9, NLT

BEFORE MY WIFE AND I ever saw the interior of the house we now live in, I was ready to buy it, just because of the surrounding countryside. As we waited for the real estate agent to show up to give us a tour, I walked around the back of the house and was instantly sold, ready to sign on the dotted line, regardless of what we might find on the inside. Fortunately, we liked what we saw, and God has truly blessed us with a great home.

This morning, with a cup of coffee in my hand, I sat in my favorite chair, looking out toward the hills behind the house. I still love that view. But as I was nursing my java, a cold, wet fog began rolling in, and in no time at all my view was obstructed. What moments before had been awesome and beautiful quickly became a white mass of nothing. It happens. I live in the Pacific Northwest, and the weather—especially in the winter—can change pretty rapidly and dramatically.

Here's what struck me: The hills in all their splendor were still there, but my view of them had changed. If I'd had X-ray vision, I would still have been able to see everything just as it was; but because I have normal vision and no superpowers that I know of, I had a diminished perspective.

Life is that way. At best, we humans have a three-dimensional ability to see the world around us. Even someone with 20/20 vision can't see very far in the dark or through a deep fog. Our vision is limited. It is restricted by our humanness on the one hand and by circumstances beyond our control on the other. Of course, we all know this. It's a basic biological fact that we have physical limitations. Why is it, then, that we are so surprised when things sneak up on us? Why is it we're so easily blown away by circumstances and trials that seem to come out of nowhere?

My eldest daughter, Jessica, and her husband, Nate, have an adopted African American son named Caleb. I call him my chocolate grandson, and if you know how much I love chocolate, you know that is a really good thing. He is adorable, incredible, and very advanced for his age. I can't believe how much this little guy has stolen my heart.

The Bible says that we, as Christ-followers, have been adopted as sons and daughters of God (Romans 8:15). Theologically, I've understood that concept for a long time. Relationally, I am just now beginning to truly understand what it means.

God has fully and absolutely accepted and embraced us as his kids. As much as the Jews have been his children for millennia, through Christ we are now his sons and daughters forever. There are no second-class citizens in God's Kingdom. We are not forced to fly coach while others fly first class. We all have equal value and importance to our heavenly Father. Amazing and true.

Not once have I ever looked at Caleb and thought, *Well, he's just adopted, not really flesh of my flesh or bone of my bone.* Never. Not at all. He is and always will be as much a grandson to me as any of my other grandchildren. He is a gift to our family and a joy beyond description. God has put him in my heart just as I am in God's heart. Thanks to my grandson Caleb, I now understand my adoption into the family of God better than I ever did before.

Let me tell you how Caleb came to be a part of our family.

Jessica and Nate wanted to be parents more than just about anything else. If you had asked my daughter as a child what she wanted to be when she grew up, she would have said, "A mommy." She has always had the smarts and the drive to accomplish whatever she wanted to accomplish. She easily could have become a doctor, a brilliant physicist, or a Harvard professor. As a teenager, she was quite skilled at making an argument. (Boy, is that an understatement.) And because of her strong debating skills, I often wondered if she might become a successful attorney someday. She graduated from high school as valedictorian and could have gone to college anywhere. (I'm biased, of course. I'm a dad, and a proud one at that.) The one longing, however, that remained Jessica's constant and greatest desire was to be a wife and mother.

One night after Nate and Jess had been married for a couple of years, our doorbell rang. When I opened the door, my daughter practically leapt into my arms.

"I'm pregnant!"

I've never seen her more excited or with a bigger smile across her beautiful face. Her dream was coming true; a baby was on the way. I was thrilled for her and Nate. The joy of being a parent and grandparent is unsurpassed, in my opinion. Children truly are a gift from the Lord. We laughed together and looked forward with great anticipation to the birth of another baby into our growing clan.

A few weeks later, we were all devastated when Jess miscarried and lost the baby. I couldn't believe it.

"God, where are you in all of this? How could you let this happen? All my little girl wants is to be a mommy, and this is too much to bear."

Tragically, miscarriages are fairly common. Sources vary, but many estimates suggest that approximately one in four pregnancies ends in miscarriage, and some think that the number could be as high as one in three. If you include loss that occurs before a positive pregnancy test, some researchers believe that 40 percent of all conceptions result in loss. Those are not just numbers, by the way, they are real lives lost. And they leave real parents, with real dreams, facing horrible heartbreak.

Like you, I've known quite a few women who seem to get pregnant without even trying. But Jess and Nate had tried for some time, and now this; it shattered our world.

To their credit, Nate and Jess took their heartache and pain to the One who knows it best—to the One who lost his own Son. Over time, healing came, but no more pregnancies. It appeared that now they would have to deal with the realities of infertility.

As a son, brother, and husband, I've had to deal with plenty of personal heartache. But as a father, nothing eats my lunch more or rips my heart to shreds faster than to see my children suffer. I would give anything to spare my kids the pain they have gone through.

At times, I think I get a small glimpse into the Father-heart of God for us. If, as a human father, I love my kids enough to do anything for them, how much more does God love us? No wonder he gave his one and only Son for us. God's love and grace truly are epic.

In the same chapter in which the apostle Paul writes about our adoption as children of God, he expounds in ecstasy about the unstoppable, unmovable love of God for us. And then he makes this amazing statement: "What, then, shall we say in response to these things? If God is for us, who can be against us? He who did not spare his own Son, but gave him up for us all—how will he not also, along with him, graciously give us all things?" (Romans 8:31-32).

God loves you and me so much that he did not spare even his own Son for us; therefore, we can believe that there is nothing good our loving Father will hold back from his kids. I know this is true. I know this is the heart of God for us. I know all of this, but my faith was shaken pretty hard through this loss.

When a cold, miserable, deep, and blinding fog enters your world, it's hard to see beyond the pain. It's hard to trust that God is good. It's hard to get past your agony, your loss, and your overwhelming sorrow. It feels a lot like you have been blindfolded and told to walk along the edge of the Grand Canyon. It's scary. It can be very hard to keep walking when you're afraid of plunging to your death, with a single wrong step, into a chasm of darkness below. Well-meaning people will say, "Just trust and obey, for there's no other way to be happy in Jesus, but to trust and obey." For the record, I love the old song that contains those words as its chorus. It's just that when a person is hurting, those lyrics can come across as flippantly cliché.

I want to scream, "Get away from me! I don't need your plastic-Jesus platitudes!"

I *know* I need to trust. I *know* God's grace is sufficient. I just wish I could see what's going on. Emotional and spiritual blindness is crushing to the soul.

The Day He Came

After trying for quite a while to get pregnant again, Jess and Nate began to consider adoption. They contacted a Christian agency and began the detailed process of completing background checks, a home study, and a mound of paperwork.

The agency told them it could take anywhere from a few months to a few years to receive a child. Within a matter of weeks, however, a birth mom chose them to be the parents of her child. When the kids called with the news, we were all thrilled. Our mourning was turning to laughter and joy once again.

All we knew at first was that it was a boy and he was African American. Nate and Jess had made it clear that they were willing to have a child of any ethnicity and either sex. That, in part, probably explained why things happened so quickly for them, but it was obvious to all of us that God was doing something amazing.

The birth mom was on the other side of the state, but when Jess and Nate got the call that she was in labor, they dropped everything and hit the road. A Northwest blizzard could not have held them back. They were going to pick up their son! Did I mention that my daughter is pretty driven?

About an hour later, somewhere on I-90 near a little town called Ritzville, they got a call from the adoption agency. Seeing that number on their phone must have given them at least a second or two of panic. *What if the birth mom has changed her mind? What if something happened to the baby during the delivery?*

When we have hoped and dreamed for something for so long, often there is a part of us that feels like it is never going to happen, like something always ends up mucking up the gears.

The call was to inform them that the little boy had arrived, but also to let them know he had been born with a cleft lip. The agency rep said, "We'll understand if you want to back out of this adoption."

I am so proud of Nate and Jess. Without hesitation they said, "Are you kidding? None of that matters. We're on our way to get our baby!"

Three days later, they were on their way home with Caleb, and within minutes of their arrival in Spokane, Grandpa was holding his newest little grandson. I truly am at a loss to describe how much I love Caleb William Scott Harris (William is *my* middle name, by the way). I imagine that someday he might read this, and I can only hope and pray that he knows how deeply he is loved.

Back to my favorite cup of joe, my favorite chair, and my favorite view . . .

As I was sitting there, it dawned on me: I never saw this coming. Without the miscarriage, there might never have been a Caleb in our lives.

If Jess had carried her first child to full term, she and Nate might still have adopted a child someday. It was something they had always considered. But the timing would have precluded the entrance of Caleb into *our* family. He still would have been born, and some other lucky couple would be his parents today. But he is a priceless part of our family because of something horrible and heartbreaking. The loss of one baby brought another one into our lives.

I didn't see that coming.

Our perspective is so limited. Our vision is so imperfect. Our ability to see the bigger picture is incredibly restricted and inadequate. We live so often in a fog. The hills are still there, but we can't see them. The view from God's vantage point is the same, but we are blind and afraid. Fog happens.

Imagine with me a different way to live. Imagine what our lives might be like if we truly trusted the one person who has no limitations and no vision restrictions. God sees the beginning from the end. Time is not linear to him; it's eternal. How might your life be radically different if you accepted the blindfold and then walked along the edge of the cliff knowing that God is the one who is holding your hand and guiding your path?

It hurts to lose someone or something of value.

It's hard to suffer without fear.

It kills us not to know or understand the *why* behind every challenging circumstance.

But maybe God has a plan that goes beyond our ability to figure it out. Maybe he is up to something that we can't see yet. Truth is, on this side of eternity, we may never understand it all. But maybe this side of eternity is just that—only a blip on the radar screen in the grand scale of all things eternal.

By now you know that I'm the last guy in the world to say, "Just hold it together." That is so not my point.

Agonize.

Struggle.

Wrestle with God.

Weep and wail and wonder.

But remember this . . . maybe, just maybe, there is a Caleb waiting for you.

17

DREAMS AND DARKNESS AND DEMONS! OH MY!

We don't want Satan to outsmart us.
We know how he does his evil work.

2 CORINTHIANS 2:11, NIrV

SOME WOULD SAY I'M A DREAMER. For a few, that would be a bad thing. To them, dreamers are not very down-to-earth. Dreamers tend to be too emotional and subjective. Dreamers are weird.

They would also question the necessity or validity of dreams for today. I can almost hear their argument: "We have the Word of God, and it is enough! Once upon a time God spoke to men and women through dreams, but since the completion of the Bible, dreams are no longer necessary or a means by which God speaks to his people."

For others, being a dreamer is cool. They would say a dreamer has the potential of being a great vision-caster and inspirer of people. They would quickly point to men and women throughout church history, like Martin Luther King Jr., who had a dream that changed the course of history.

The mature among this group of dream believers would never put a dream above the Scriptures, but they would contend that God still uses dreams to warn and guide his followers. They might also point out that the prophet Joel said that in the last days, God would pour out his Spirit on all people, that old men would dream dreams and young men would see visions (Joel 2:28).

I guess that makes me old, since I'm a dreamer of dreams.

Actually, we all dream every night about something. Of course, most of our dreams are human in origin and not from God. I have a friend in Florida who writes down every dream he has and spends way too much time trying to figure out what they all mean. In fact, he has a very long list of what certain images supposedly represent and uses this dream dictionary to interpret what he sees and what he thinks God is trying to say to him through his dreams.

Seriously, every dream a word from God? I don't think so.

That being said, in my humble opinion, some dreams are holy and God-given for a very important purpose in our lives.

Researchers have never really landed on a solid explanation for why we have dreams, or what purpose, if any, they serve. Some have strongly suggested that dreams serve no meaningful purpose, while others just as passionately believe that dreaming is essential to mental, emotional, and even physical well-being.

Many embrace Sigmund Freud's theory. He suggested that dreams are a depiction of our unconscious desires. Henry David Thoreau once said, "Dreams are the touchstones of our characters."

I don't have any solid answers to give you regarding why we dream. I like Thoreau's quote, but I have no idea what he was talking about. Touchstones of our characters? Whatever, dude.

Nonetheless, I know there have been times when God has powerfully grabbed my attention through a dream that smelled like, felt like, looked like, and sounded like him.

If that's too touchy-feely or weird for you, sorry. I believe in dreams and visions because I find them throughout the Bible and throughout the history of the church. I also believe God can use anything he chooses to lead, guide, and direct his children. Even dreams.

When we teach children to read, we show them simple pictures. The words below the image may say, "See Spot run." And we say to the children, "See the dog? He's running. His name is Spot. See Spot run."

That's how we talk to children. It's how we instruct very simpleminded people in a very basic way. I think it's important for us to understand that God might give us a dream, vision, or picture of something because it is the only way we can grasp what he's up to—through a simple picture. Certainly, that doesn't make us better or smarter, maybe just the opposite. In fact, dreams might be another example of God's goodness and grace to us.

He Was Big, Bad, and Powerful!

So why all this dream talk?

Last night, I had a dream. It shook me so profoundly that it woke me up. I wouldn't call it a nightmare, but it was intense enough to jar me from a sound sleep at about two in the morning.

Here's the gist of what I saw. I was with my adult siblings, and we were actively engaged in something important. I don't know exactly what we were up to, but I knew it was significant and of great consequence to many. We weren't laughing or smiling, but I sensed there was enormous joy in our endeavors. My two brothers, my sister, and I were extremely focused, driven, and passionate about the work at hand.

In the dream, I suddenly became aware of a very dark and determined presence watching us as we worked. He was huge, ugly, scary, and powerful. The look in his eyes is what I noticed first. There was a hatred and disgust for us that said it all. This entity was committed to our destruction. Imagine the disdain Darth Vader had for Han Solo, and you might come close to seeing what I saw.

It was freaky.

It was dark.

It was intimidating and menacing.

I was glad I woke up.

As I lay in bed for quite a while, wide awake, I prayed, "God, what's up? Is this a warning from you? Is there something here I need to see or understand?"

It's hard to describe how God sometimes unpacks things for me. I certainly didn't hear an audible voice, but like a teacher writing an equation out on a whiteboard for a student to grasp, God broke this dream out for me in a very clear way.

To begin with, my family members represented themselves. But I also understood that my siblings represented two other things: multiple generations of our family, perhaps many generations; and also the body of Christ, my extended family of believers. The work we were involved in with such desire, focus, joy, and passion was the work of God's Kingdom. We were serving God.

On a grander scale, the big, scary guy symbolized the forces of hell set against the Kingdom of God and all those who belong to Christ. However, as I lay there in the middle of the night, I started to think about all the broken tragedy in my own family's history.

Two of my grandfather's siblings, a brother and a sister, were convicted of murder in the 1940s. The story goes that they were thieves who brutally killed their partner over a disagreement. My great-uncle Mike was executed. My great-aunt Millie was sent to prison for life.

My grandparents' marriage was a mess, and my father and grandfather never got along. My grandparents raised three boys—my two uncles, Don and Paul, and my dad, George. Tragically, when my dad was sixteen, he was kicked out of the house and went to live with my uncle Don.

By now, you probably know enough about my parents' marriage and the family I grew up in. Words like *dysfunctional* and *broken* don't seem strong enough to describe us.

The saga continues with my brothers and sister. Divorce. Horrible failures. Bankruptcies. So far, no one has been accused of murder, but we've all made our fair share of foolish mistakes. We've been recipients of boatloads of grace, but we've also known plenty of tragedy.

As I lay in the dark staring up at the glowing red numbers on the ceiling from my atomic clock, I also reflected on all the people—tens of thousands, at least—who have been positively and powerfully affected by the godly heritage I have in my family.

My uncle Don was an amazing man. He was gifted and greatly used by God. He was a successful pastor, an author, a contributing editor to *Leadership* magazine, a world-traveling speaker, and a seminary adjunct professor. The influence of his life has touched thousands and thousands, and continues to do so even after his death in 2011.

My uncle Paul was also remarkable. He was a missionary in Vietnam, a thriving pastor, and an author as well. He was once a seminary chancellor, and he was the president of a large denomination when he passed away. The ripples of his life have touched incredible numbers of people throughout the world.

My dad, messed up as he was, was still considered by both of his brothers to be the most creative of the brothers Bubna and a better speaker than either of them. It's crazy, I know, but I still get cards and e-mails from time to time from people all over the country who say, "Your dad was the best pastor I ever had; I am what I am today because of his ministry." That is God's epic grace at work through a broken vessel.

I could go on and bore you with many more examples. I haven't even touched the Cole side of my family (my mother's side) and literally hundreds of other stories about the phenomenal heritage I have in Christ through aunts and uncles who have served our country and served the Kingdom of God with unbelievable courage and achievement.

I really don't want to sound like I'm bragging, but despite the glaring and tragic deficiencies in my pedigree, I have grown up among giants. My aunts and uncles are heroes to me and to thousands and thousands of others.

Though Satan is not omniscient (all-knowing), is it possible he saw a bloodline that posed a significant threat to his kingdom and his power? Is it possible he determined to do everything within his demonic power to destroy a family? Could it be that even the premature deaths of so many in my family history are the direct result of a frontal assault by the enemy?

Good grief, how could you look at my family history—the good, the bad, and the ugly—and not see it? We aren't special, no more so than any other family who loves the cause of Christ. But without question, the spiritual battle has raged for a long time in my tribe.

The apostle Paul writes in Ephesians 6:12-13, "Our struggle is not against flesh and blood, but against the rulers, against the authorities, against the powers of this dark world and against the spiritual forces of evil in the heavenly realms. Therefore put on the full armor of God, so that when the day of evil comes, you may be able to stand your ground, and after you have done everything, to stand."

Paul made it clear there is a battle raging all around us; it is not a battle against humans, but a war against dark forces of evil.

We don't like to think about this reality.

We don't like it when we're confronted with darkness.

It seems a lot less weird to simply focus on the broken human part of our world.

But whether we like it or not, see it or not, or believe it or not, the battle still rages and absolutely crusades against us throughout generations.

If you stop and think about it, I bet there is a common dark struggle that you can see throughout your own family history.

Substance abuse.

Serious anger management issues.

Infidelity.

Maybe everything from crippling fear to chronic failures.

The battle rages.

So what's the point of all of this? Why a chapter on dreams and demons and spiritual warfare? Because every time you and I forget that we have an enemy, we risk getting blasted in the battle and taken out by our adversary. Every idiotic thing I've done can be traced back to either forgetting who I am in Christ or forgetting that I am in the thick of the battle on this planet for the sake of Christ.

The dream I had last night did not teach me anything I didn't already know about spiritual warfare. What it did was vividly remind me of a critical reality. We are at war! We cannot afford to wander through this life in ignorance. We need to put on the full armor of God *daily* so that we can stand our ground.

We do not need to live in fear. Our King is victor, and "the one who is in you is greater than the one who is in the world" (1 John 4:4). But we cannot afford to live in unawareness of our desperate need to pray hard, to solemnly guard our hearts with God's truth, and to lock arms with our brothers and sisters as we hold up the shield of faith.

Whether we are a casualty of war or a conqueror in Christ has a lot to do with our alertness to the darkness that lurks all around us, and our awareness of the malicious schemes of the evil one.

Be wise. Be aware. Be strong in the Lord and in the power of his might. And the next time you have a dream, if it wakes you up to something you needed to see, thank God, and dream on, baby—dream on.

18

BUSHWHACKED!

O Sovereign LORD! You made the heavens and earth by your
strong hand and powerful arm. Nothing is too hard for you!

JEREMIAH 32:17, NLT

USE YOUR GOD-GIVEN IMAGINATION and take a walk with
me. Picture the most beautiful beach you've ever seen or
graced with your presence. Maybe it's a long, stunning strip
of paradise with glimmering white sand and gentle waves lap-
ping at its edge. Bordering the beach is a tropical forest of
gorgeous palm trees with the sound of exotic birds echoing
through the lush jungle. From the center of this island dream-
land, mountains rise to the sky, teasing the clouds with their
majestic glory, and a brilliant rainbow—make that a double
rainbow—pierces through the biggest thunderheads you've
ever seen. On the beach, the sun is perfect. Not too hot. Not
too intense. And the wind is gently caressing your face and
body with a whisper of jasmine in the air. Got it? It's heaven
on earth!

Now imagine the exact opposite (sorry), and you will see

the beach of nightmares my family experienced one summer many years ago.

The Oregon coast, in many ways, is some of the most beautiful coastland in America. But the beaches can be extremely cold and windy. Most of the Northwest coastline consists of jagged cliffs and lots of weather-beaten rocks covered with bird droppings. I don't think there's a mile of beach anywhere in Oregon that sees more than a couple months of sunshine a year. The average temperature is right around fifty degrees, the water is beyond frigid, and the waves violently assault the shore. On top of that, there's the occasional aroma of a dead and rotting sea lion that fills the air with a vile stench. Got it? Not so much a heaven on earth!

One Saturday, Laura and I decided to take the kids to the coast. (We lived in Portland at the time). The beach was only about an hour or two from our home, and it could be a fun place to hang out. The goal was to experience some much-needed quality family time.

In addition to our own two who were still living at home, we had a young Russian boy named Alex who was living with us. He was about ten years old, and he was quite a challenge. Because his mother was a drug addict, his grandmother had custody, but she had asked us to take Alex into our home for a season to see if we could help him.

We arrived in the little beachfront community of Seaside just as the rain stopped. Because it was a Saturday in the middle of the summer (I use the word *summer* loosely), the streets were jammed with tourists and ocean-loving Oregonians like us.

Normally, we'd walk around town, head over to the boardwalk or the aquarium, and then maybe spend some time flying kites on the beach. But today the overwhelming crowds drove us to a place called Elmer Feldenheimer State Natural Area, just south of Seaside.

We thought, *This is a great day for a hike. Let's take the kids on a fun adventure!* Little did we know what we were getting ourselves into.

As you might imagine, the kids were less than thrilled with the idea of a hike. They wanted to ride the bumper cars in town, fly kites, and consume large quantities of deep-fried elephant ears. Alex was the most vocal; a walk in the woods was not at all what he had in mind.

I told them, "Hey, this will be a great family activity. Let's experience something new and beautiful. It'll be fun!" They groaned and resigned themselves to go along, only because they didn't have a choice.

We parked the car in a small lot at the north end of the park entrance and headed south on an exceptionally well-marked trail through some extremely dense forest. Everything was terribly wet. About a hundred inches of rain drench this park on an annual basis. Taking a walk just after a storm made the conditions something like walking through a swamp. It was muddy, cold, dark, and pretty miserable. The trail twists and turns like a nasty roller coaster through mile after mile of hills and relatively untouched coastal wilderness.

No Porta-Potties.

No Starbucks coffee.

No deep-fried elephant ears.

Just woods and ferns and lots of overgrown, thorny blackberry bushes.

I wish I could tell you that my kids relished the journey. I truly wish I could tell you that they embraced the expedition. I certainly wish I could tell you that they were little troupers who trudged on with the attitude of a Navy SEAL. I would have settled for the outlook of a Boy Scout. But in reality, they griped and moaned the entire time.

"Dad, this isn't fun!"

"Dad, let's go back."

"Mom, please *make* Dad stop!"

Frankly, I wasn't having that much fun either, but I was determined to finish what we had started. "Stay the course" was my mantra.

There was just one itsy-bitsy little problem. I didn't know where the trail was leading us, let alone where (or if) it ended. In short, I had no idea where we were headed.

Finally, after what seemed like hours of complaints, I made an executive decision. Apparently, the trail *had* no end, so I decided the smart thing to do was to go off trail and head west to the beach. (Actually, the smart thing to do would have been to turn around and go back the way we'd come, but that didn't sound especially adventurous to me.) My thinking went like this: *West will take us to the beach; hiking along the beach will be a lot easier than going up and down through miles of wet forest; the beach is beautiful, and the kids will be thrilled.*

Did I mention that the Oregon coastline is some of the roughest terrain on the planet? Jagged cliffs; huge, weather-beaten, slippery rocks covered in bird guano; waves big and strong enough to crush a full-grown man to death; wind that blows sand so hard it grates on your face like sandpaper. *What was I thinking?*

Furthermore, when we left the well-marked, open, clear trail to bushwhack our way out to the beach, vicious child-eating blackberry bushes and ferns attacked us. Whatever part of our bodies had been dry up to that point ended up entirely soaked.

It was horrible.

When we finally arrived on the shore, there wasn't much of a beach to walk on. I said out loud, "Maybe we should go back up the hill and find the trail." In unison, they all said, "No way!" Alex said something in Russian: "Вы идиот!" I'm pretty sure he was cursing me, or the day I was born, or saying something else fairly horrible.

So we headed north along the coast. As we scrambled over rocks, attempted to avoid the powerful and frigid waves, and made our way along the bottom of some extremely steep and imposing cliffs, I kept saying, "Well, we wanted an adventure, and we sure got one!" No one was amused. In fact, at that moment, I was the least popular dad on the planet.

Adventure was becoming a four-letter word to my family.

Eventually, we came to a point where I knew the parking lot was just to the east of us. The problem was getting there, because the cliff was in our way. After some reconnaissance with my youngest son, we found a way to climb the cliff and reach our final destination. But the climb scared the dickens out of my wife and Alex, both of whom are afraid of heights. Rock climbing was exhausting, dirty, and scary. I went from least popular dad to biggest idiot pretty quickly.

Hours later—fatigued, grumpy, cold, and wet—we climbed into the car, and I said it one more time just for effect: "What an adventure!"

Their silence spoke volumes.

The two-hour drive home was quiet as the kids and my wife

collapsed in a pool of drool. Sleep brought some comfort, but still no joy. I had a lot of time to think and reflect on what had happened that day.

My intentions were noble. I truly believed a hike would be fun and provide the much-loved quality family time I longed for. I didn't take them on that journey out of coldhearted meanness (though they would have argued differently). All I wanted was to be together. To talk. To laugh. To enjoy each other's company. To build a fond memory through a fun bonding experience.

Here are some things I realized on that long, quiet ride home—and it wasn't about bushwhacking or getting lost. Then again, maybe it was. You see, parenting can be tough at times, and we often feel as if we've lost our way.

Sometimes we parents have the best of intentions as we lead our little troops forward into adulthood, but things don't turn out like we planned or hoped. We make hundreds of decisions all the time, and typically we are genuinely trying to make the right decision for our families. More often than not, we're attempting to do the best we can with what we've got. But all too often, it seems, what we hoped would be a delightful walk along the beach ends up being a nightmare on Elm Street.

We make an unwise financial decision and our family suffers the consequences.

We choose to go in a direction that ends in disaster.

We create a relational issue that destroys trust and confidence.

We cause heartache and despair instead of inspiring joy and faith.

Isn't it shocking how one bad decision often cascades into a whole brush-busting journey of anguish?

KURT W. BUBNA

The Bible says, "There is a path before each person that seems right, but it ends in death" (Proverbs 14:12, NLT). Boy, does that describe our day at Feldenheimer!

I felt awful about the condition of my family on the way home from Seaside. The more I thought about it, the worse I felt. Stupid thoughts like, *They'd be better off without me* kept circling my mind like buzzards over a dead carcass.

At about that moment, we went through a tunnel on the route home. As we entered the relative darkness of that mountain tunnel, here's what the Lord spoke to my heart: *In your journey as a parent, sometimes you will enter into a dark and unfamiliar place, sometimes you will take the wrong path, sometimes you will disappoint and fail your children. Rest easy, my son, for even there in that hard place I will be with you, and I am still working.*

I was overwhelmed by God's epic grace in that tunnel. Facing my failures as a father, without condemnation from *the* Father, flooded my soul with hope.

The Blame Game

Years ago, when I was on staff at a large church, a mother came to me in utter despair. Her fifteen-year-old daughter was pregnant. That would be difficult enough for any parent to deal with, but the fact that the man responsible for her daughter's condition was the woman's third (and current) husband was too much to bear. Adding to this tragic mess was the daughter's addiction to methamphetamine.

How would you feel if you found out that your drug-plagued teenage daughter had been impregnated by your husband, her stepfather? Like this mother, you'd probably feel responsible to some degree. "I brought that man into my home. I should have protected my daughter. I'm responsible for this chaos!"

I took my kids on a bad hike through some awful terrain. Compared to my experience, the woman's was far worse, and perhaps your story is heartrending and tragic, as well. The reality is, regardless of the depth of our family struggles, we parents often carry a heavy burden of guilt over the condition of our children. When things go terribly wrong, and especially when it's in our homes and with our families, it's normal to condemn ourselves and beat ourselves up. Who else are we going to blame? But deliberately punishing ourselves with blame and shame, instead of turning toward the epic grace of God, *never* produces anything good.

Of course we fail. Of course we go the wrong direction. Of course we go off the beaten path too often. But the promise of the Perfect Dad is that he will always be with us, and he is always working. Our part is to trust in a God who understands our humanity, our tendency to fail, and our need for his endless grace.

King David, who had his own serious parenting challenges, wrote these words in Psalm 103:13-14: "As a father has compassion on his children, so the LORD has compassion on those who fear him; for he knows how we are formed, he remembers that we are dust."

God knows how we blow it as parents from time to time. He understands us. And rather than beat us up, he offers compassion, comfort, and help.

How about you? Have you ever felt as if you've royally screwed up? Have you ever beaten yourself up thinking, *I've messed up my kids and I'm to blame for their sins?* Have you ever lain in bed at night stressing out over the impact of your idiotic decisions on the ones you love? Have you ever thought to yourself, *I am being pummeled by enormous waves of failure that are waaayyyy too strong for my pathetic little parenting skills?*

Of course, you've felt that way. We *all* have.

But here's what matters most: hope, faith, and love.

Hope in a God who can take our mistakes and redeem anything surrendered to him.

Faith in a God who is bigger than our failures, no matter what they are.

Love from a Father who will *never* give up on us and wants us *never* to give up on him.

Be the best parent you can be. When you screw up, own it. Learn from your mistakes. Humbly acknowledge your weakness on a regular basis to God, to your spouse, and to your kids: "I am a flawed human being who needs a ton of grace and a boatload of forgiveness on a regular basis."

And by the way, don't listen to the accusing voice of the evil one, who never has your best interest in mind. Don't go there. It's a fruitless endeavor designed to demoralize you. You are never truly lost in a wilderness, even though you might feel like it, because God has your back and he is always with you.

By now, I hope you've heard in my words a deep conviction that *nothing* is too hard, and *no one* too far gone, for God to redeem, restore, or renew.

Not you.

Not your family.

Not now.

Not ever.

19

THE PROBLEM WITH EXPECTATIONS

Bear with each other and forgive one another if any of you has
a grievance against someone. Forgive as the Lord forgave you.
And over all these virtues put on love, which binds them all together
in perfect unity. Let the peace of Christ rule in your hearts, since as
members of one body you were called to peace. And be thankful.

COLOSSIANS 3:13-15

THINK ABOUT THE LAST TIME you had a conflict with someone. Got it? I'm willing to bet that at the heart of that conflict was an unmet expectation.

We expect our spouse to treat us nicely. If he or she doesn't, baby, there is conflict.

We want our friends to watch our backs and protect us from getting blindsided by an enemy. When they don't, there's trouble.

We expect our kids to appreciate all that we do for them. When they don't, we get frustrated.

Expectations. Everybody has them, but when ours get ignored or trashed, we go ballistic. I've seen people live long and bitter lives full of anger and toxic hate because they've never learned how to process the unavoidable reality of unmet expectations.

I've seen others become depressed, withdrawn, and even suicidal because they have simply given up on people and life due to a whole boatload of unmet expectations.

Road Trip with Grandma

Years ago, before my wife and I were even married, we took a vacation together with her grandmother. First let me be clear—we slept in separate beds, and her grandmother was always in the same room. I might have been a typical teenager, but come on, there's not much you can get away with when Grandma is watching.

We drove Grandma's van from Southern California to Oregon and back. She was about four-foot-nothing, old, and not the best driver, so I did most of the driving. The first couple of days went great. We were all fresh and excited about the adventure. Grandma was a little nervous about having me behind the wheel, but I generally took it slow and easy and assured her I was a great driver. I neglected to mention that I had received three speeding tickets in the past two years. But I figured what she didn't know couldn't hurt me.

Things started to get pretty tense, however, on the third day of the trip. We had just gone over the mountain passes, and she thought I was driving too close to the edge at times. The first time she brought it up, I just smiled and said, "Grandma, I'm keeping it between the lines; it just looks like we're closer to the edge" (*because you're blind as a bat*, I thought).

She disagreed and wasn't happy, but seemed to accept my explanation until the next time she thought I was too close to the edge, and then the crazy cycle started all over again.

A much more aggressive critique of my driving skills came when we encountered some serious traffic on I-5 near Eugene. According to Grandma, I was tailgating, and I should stay out of the fast lane anyway because otherwise we might miss our exit. Our next exit was in Portland, which was still about a hundred miles to the north. All the same, it was her van, she was paying for the gas, and I didn't want her to have a heart attack, so I obliged and moved over to the very slow lane.

The ugly climax came the following day when she told me she didn't want me eating or drinking while I was driving. It was like she'd had the worst nightmare of her life about us crashing because I had a candy bar in my mouth behind the wheel. Grandma was freakin' out.

She wasn't concerned that I might be distracted. (This was before cell phones.) And it wasn't because she didn't want me getting crumbs on her seat. It was because she was convinced I would choke while driving and kill us all in the process.

I lost it. At that point I'd had enough. We still had at least two more days in the van to get home. If she thought I was going to put down my Snickers, Cheetos, and Dr Pepper, she was crazy.

Grandma expected compliance because it was her van, her gas, and her life at risk. I expected sanity. The result? Unmet expectations and nasty conflict.

I said some things to her that I sincerely regretted later, all of which pretty much ruined the trip for everybody—especially my wife-to-be who had been putting up with both of us. In hindsight, I realize I was an idiot. Right or wrong, reasonable or unreasonable, it was her van and I should have honored her requests.

Unmet expectations. They're everywhere.

I've got a friend who is about forty-eight now, and he's had about that many jobs in his life. He's smart and well educated. He's a hard worker. He's a likable guy, yet he either quits or gets fired from jobs on a way-too-regular basis.

Here's his pattern. He finds a great job. He gets excited. Then he finds out that his boss or coworkers are human and gets frustrated. Next thing I know, he's looking for another great job. The problem? He has unrealistic and unmet expectations.

You probably know at least one person who goes through spouses the same way my friend goes through jobs. They find "the love of their life . . . their soul mate," fall madly in love, and then get married, probably a bit too quickly. Then they discover—shock of all shocks—that their spouse is human and far from perfect. The little things that didn't matter before really start to matter now. The unmet expectations start to pile up and they think, *This stinks! I'm out of here!*

Next thing you know, they've fallen out of love with the (former) love of their life and they're looking for love again in all the wrong places.

Unmet expectations, realistic or not, are at the heart of just about every broken relationship.

Let me shift gears for a moment and go biblical on you. If what I've suggested is true, are there any examples of this problem in the Bible?

So glad you asked. Where do I begin?

How about with the story of Cain and Abel? Two brothers. Two sacrifices. Two expectations that God would find their offerings acceptable. But one is good, the other is not.

Genesis 4:5 says, "Cain was very angry, and his face was downcast." Cain was so angry, in fact, that he killed his own brother. In this case, an unmet expectation led to a horrible and tragic act of murder.

How about Abraham and Sarah? (Known as Abram and Sarai before God changed their names.) Here's just one of the examples from their lives:

Now there was a famine in the land, and Abram went down to Egypt to live there for a while because the famine was severe. As he was about to enter Egypt, he said to his wife Sarai, "I know what a beautiful woman you are. When the Egyptians see you, they will say, 'This is his wife.' Then they will kill me but will let you live. Say you are my sister, so that I will be treated well for your sake and my life will be spared because of you."

When Abram came to Egypt, the Egyptians saw that she was a very beautiful woman. And when Pharaoh's officials saw her, they praised her to Pharaoh, and she was taken into his palace. He treated Abram well for her sake, and Abram acquired sheep and cattle, male and female donkeys, menservants and maidservants, and camels.

But the LORD inflicted serious diseases on Pharaoh and his household because of Abram's wife Sarai. So Pharaoh summoned Abram. "What have you done to me?" he said. "Why didn't you tell me she was your wife? Why did you say, 'She is my sister,' so that I took her to be my wife? Now then, here is your wife. Take her and go!" Then Pharaoh gave orders about Abram to his men, and they sent him on his way, with his wife and everything he had. GENESIS 12:10-20

Abraham had been driven to Egypt out of hunger because there was a severe famine in the land of Canaan. Knowing that his wife, Sarah, was a babe, he expected trouble: "Once that nasty old Pharaoh gets a look at her, I'm toast!" He convinced Sarah to lie, which only complicated things, and sure enough, Sarah ended up being groomed for Pharaoh's harem. Then all sorts of trouble in the form of serious diseases hit Pharaoh and his clan. God intervened and saved the day, but Abraham and Sarah got deported.

Abraham expected to be killed. Pharaoh expected to be told the truth and expected to add another beauty to his harem. The end result: conflict. Abraham was fortunate that God had his back or he would have had his worst fears come true—death at the hands of the Egyptians.

What about our expectations of God? What happens when we expect God to do something and things don't go the way we want?

Score: Elijah 450, Prophets of Baal 0

I love the stories of Elijah in the Scriptures. This great prophet of God was a mighty man who did incredible acts in the name of Jehovah. But things didn't always go the way he expected.

In 1 Kings 18, Elijah goes to Mount Carmel for a major-league smackdown of 450 prophets of Baal. At Elijah's request, God shows up with fire—a lot of fire—and consumes a water-drenched sacrifice. The people of Israel realize that the Lord God is sovereign (duh!) and then Elijah orders the execution of the 450 false prophets.

Great story. Serious drama, conflict, and then the good guy beats the bad guys. God wins.

In the very next chapter, however, things take an interesting twist:

> Now Ahab told Jezebel everything Elijah had done
> and how he had killed all the prophets with the sword.
> So Jezebel sent a messenger to Elijah to say, "May the
> gods deal with me, be it ever so severely, if by this time
> tomorrow I do not make your life like that of one
> of them."
>
> Elijah was afraid and ran for his life. When he came
> to Beersheba in Judah, he left his servant there, while
> he himself went a day's journey into the desert. He
> came to a broom tree, sat down under it and prayed
> that he might die. "I have had enough, LORD," he said.
> "Take my life; I am no better than my ancestors." Then
> he lay down under the tree and fell asleep.
>
> I KINGS 19:1-5

King Ahab tells Queen Jezebel the bad news: All your priests are dead at the hands of Elijah. Apparently, the queen was not a woman to be messed with, so Elijah gets out of Dodge as quickly as he can. Afraid for his life, he ends up depressed and whining, "God, just take me out. I can't do this anymore." Then he does what a lot of people do when depressed—he zones out. Ever been there? I have. When the pressure's on, sometimes all we want to do is sleep . . . or eat . . . or self-medicate with television or booze or drugs or an illicit relationship. Or we simply disengage and run away emotionally.

Elijah's story takes a turn for the better, though. An angel shows up to fix him breakfast (now that would be cool), he is strengthened, and later he has an amazing encounter with God at Horeb, the mountain of God, but that's another story. What's interesting to me is that, even after God sends an angel to help him—*think* about that!—Elijah is still hung up on his unmet expectations.

> [Elijah] got up and ate and drank. Strengthened by that food, he traveled forty days and forty nights until he reached Horeb, the mountain of God. There he went into a cave and spent the night.
>
> And the word of the LORD came to him: "What are you doing here, Elijah?"
>
> He replied, "I have been very zealous for the LORD God Almighty. The Israelites have rejected your covenant, broken down your altars, and put your prophets to death with the sword. I am the only one left, and now they are trying to kill me too."
>
> 1 KINGS 19:8-10

In other words, "God, I've done everything you've asked me to do; why aren't you taking better care of me?" Elijah had unmet expectations of God, and it led to some pretty serious inner conflict and disappointment with God.

Here's the question, though: Why did Elijah get discouraged and depressed in the first place? Remember, he had just seen the overwhelming power and faithfulness of God in action—*firsthand*. So why did he run? Why didn't he reply to Jezebel, "Oh yeah? Bring it on, sister!"? I think it's because God didn't meet his expectations. (There's that word again.) I think Elijah believed he had done everything he could possibly do for God, and now he wanted God to once-and-for-all *eliminate* his problems, including his problem with Ahab and Jezebel.

But that's not always how God operates. Elijah could realistically expect that God would continue to care for and protect him, but it was unrealistic to expect that everything would be taken care of just the way he thought it should be. Still, it's rather stunning that Elijah could so quickly and easily forget the goodness and grace of God, which had been proven over and over again in his life.

Does that sound familiar?

Why do we do that?

Why are we so fragile and so forgetful? Perhaps it's because we tend to pull away from other people when the going gets tough. Maybe it's because we tend to lose perspective when we get frustrated or disappointed with God or others.

What was the first thing Elijah did when he got discouraged, depressed, and afraid? He ran away and isolated himself. When things didn't go exactly the way *he* wanted them to, he sat down in a dark cave and had a pity party. Not a pretty picture.

So God said, "Seriously, Elijah? What are you thinkin'?" (1 Kings 19:9, my paraphrase). I imagine Elijah shrugging his shoulders as he tries to justify his dissatisfaction with God.

Unmet expectations—whether of God or of other people—can be tough to deal with. But that's why we need each other. We need to remind one another—and be reminded—of God's power, faithfulness, and care, not to mention his epic grace. Alone, we become too self-focused and end up in despair, but together in community, we can find clarity of heart and mind.

The Long and Winding Road

I've had unmet expectations of God in my life too. As mentioned earlier, I spent the better part of my late twenties and early thirties working in the banking industry. At the end of that time, I was bivocational, working as both a pastor and a banker. The early years were tough on me. After my prodigal season was over and I was back with God, I figured I'd be back in full-time vocational ministry in no time. I expected God to restore me quickly and with flair. From my perspective, I was wasting time in the business world because I was made and called to pastor.

If you work in business, don't be offended by that statement. As I mentioned before, more people are called to utilize their God-given resources, gifts, and abilities in the business world, or in other pursuits, than are called to pastoral ministry. And God uses us fully wherever he calls us. I was just convinced that he had called me to pastor and I was impatient with the slow track of restoration and reequipping he seemed to have me on.

Bottom line, I expected God to put me back in pastoral ministry far faster than he did. Every day was a struggle for me. Every day I wondered, *How long, God? How much more of this do I have to put up with?*

My last job in banking was with a savings and loan in north San Diego County. I was a loan officer in a local branch. The job was quite a step down from my previous banking positions, but it was the only job I could get in a depressed economy.

The manager and people I worked with were awesome. They were friendly, fun, and easy-to-get-along-with folks. Nevertheless, making car loans and second mortgage loans to people, many of whom should not have been taking out loans, was extremely difficult for me. It was also a commission-only job requiring long hours and lots of paperwork.

I can't tell you how many times I drove to work, pulled in the parking lot, and had to wipe tears from my face before I got out of the car. "God, I hate this job. I don't get it. Why am I here?"

I was whining. Complaining. Murmuring. It was all about me.

As long as I was focused on my unmet expectations and my disappointment with God, life was pretty miserable.

What I failed to see was that God's plan was unfolding right on schedule. He was working on my character. He was teaching me to trust him. He was developing my patience. And most important, he was teaching me how to bloom where I was planted—that I didn't have to be in the pulpit or in the parish to exercise my calling. He put me in that branch for a reason. He wanted me to shine his light right where I was.

I remember the day I finally figured it out. I was working with a young couple who desperately wanted to buy a car that they really couldn't afford. They barely qualified for the loan, and it would have put them at their financial limits without any margin.

When they came in to sign the final documents and get their check, I asked if I could share my opinion with them. They said, "Sure!" and so I did.

"Listen, guys," I said, "I know you really want this car. I know you've provided everything I've asked for to get you qualified by our bank. I also need you to know that I get paid by commission. But here's my concern: I don't think you should take out this loan. It's a mistake." (Fortunately, my boss, who sat right next to me, was on a break and didn't hear me undercut my own sale.)

What happened next blew me away. The couple looked at

each other, the husband breathed a sigh of relief, and the wife started to cry. Then they said, "You have no idea how relieved we are to hear you say that. We've been having all sorts of second thoughts. Thanks for caring enough about us to tell us the truth." We tore up the documents and off they went, without the money and without any additional debt.

I was dumbfounded by my own actions. Did I just tell these people not to take any money from the bank when it was my job—and my source of income—to get people into loans?

I took a walk on my lunch break that day. It was a gorgeous Southern California day—sunny, warm, and windy. On my walk, I prayed, "God, I guess there's more to this job than I realized. I guess there's a reason why I'm here. (Go figure, it's not all about me.) So help me do this job well and in a way that always honors you and cares for people."

That month I earned the single largest commission check I'd ever seen. In fact, it was the largest commission paid to any loan officer in the entire county. And I can honestly say I felt pretty good about most of the loans I made.

God is so amazing. He is so full of grace.

But that's not the end of the story. About two months later, I got the job offer of my dreams, when the pastor of the church we attended came to me and said the words I'd been waiting such a long time to hear: "Hey, Kurt, I'd like you to pray about coming on staff with me as an assistant pastor."

"Are you kidding!" I said. "I've been praying about this for almost ten years. I'm in—all in! When do I start?"

God and his timing are always amazing. When will I ever learn?

God had taken me on a long and winding road, but it was his road, and in the end, I realized it was the best road for me.

Sometimes you may feel as if God has let you down. Maybe you've had perfectly reasonable expectations of him, but it seems that he's failed you. That's okay. You're in good company. Elijah, David, Jeremiah, and countless others *all* felt the same way at times.

The best thing to do is what *they* did: Cry out to God. Take your pain to him. He can handle it. Then stop, at least for a moment, and whisper through your tears, "God, I don't like this. I don't get this. Frankly, I'm mad and confused. But I choose to trust you, I choose to believe that you know all things and that you really do have a perfect plan."

We all have expectations.

We all have desires and dreams.

We all have been let down.

The call of God, however, is to forgive as we have been forgiven. As difficult sometimes as people are to live with, we need people. We need each other. And yes, we need God.

People will fail you and let you down. Love them anyway.

People will mistreat you and abuse you. Forgive them anyway.

People will say one thing and do another, breaking promises and your heart along the way. Give them grace and mercy anyway, just like God the Father has done for you.

Who is that person in your life right now? Will you become bitter or better?

The choice is yours.

20

WHAT'S LOVE GOT TO DO WITH IT?

Blessed are those whose transgressions are forgiven,
whose sins are covered. Blessed is the one whose
sin the Lord will never count against them.

ROMANS 4:7-8

FROM TIME TO TIME, I do or say something pathetically stupid that hurts or offends someone. No big surprise to you by now. I really don't mean to. It just happens, and a bit too often. When I blow it, I sometimes get depressed. Especially when I blow it in the same area over and over again.

Why did I say that again?

Why did I do that again?

Why am I such an idiot?

Everyone screws up from time to time. Everybody hurts somebody at least once in a while. As long as we're in these earth suits, it's inevitable, I suppose.

Recently, these words from the apostle Peter, who was a pretty good screwup in his own right, have meant a great deal to me: "Above all, love each other deeply, because love covers over a multitude of sins" (1 Peter 4:8).

Peter said "above all," which means this is a really big deal. This is the most important thing in our human-to-human relationships. *Love!* In fact, deep, fervent, zealous, fanatical love should be present in all of our relationships all of the time. Why? Because love covers a multitude of sins. It covers our many faults. It covers our idiocy.

Love covers everything, without exception.

I could write another book just about all the times I've hurt and wounded my dear wife. I've already told you part of our story, but let me tell you a bit more about how I learned the hard way to love my wife.

In the early years of our marriage, my unrealistic and unbiblical demands of Laura made for some really ugly moments. Like I said, almost all conflict comes from unmet expectations. I expected her to cook like Betty Crocker, handle our finances like a CPA, desire me like I was Tom Cruise (even though I'm not at all like Tom Cruise), and welcome my sexual advances at any given moment. (Of course, like most women, she's a Crock-Pot, not a microwave. I'm ready at the push of a button. She wants to savor the experience.)

Unmet expectations. Conflict. Hurtful words. Stupid actions. Amazingly, my wife loved me anyway.

I wonder how Peter learned that love covers everything, even the multitude of his sins. Was it the time he tried to talk Jesus out of going to the cross (Matthew 16:21-22)?

Was it the time he said there was no way Jesus was going to wash his feet (John 13:6-8)?

Maybe it was the time he started to sink into big-time deep water after taking his eyes off of Jesus (Matthew 14:29-30)?

I'm sure it had something to do with his denial of Jesus in

the courtyard (Luke 22:54-62) and Jesus' gracious response on the lakefront (John 21:7-18).

Peter learned a lot of things the hard way, which is why I relate to him so much, but Peter also knew the love, forgiveness, and epic grace of Jesus.

A Great Big Fish Story

After Jesus' crucifixion and resurrection, Peter, Thomas, Nathanael, James and John, and a couple of other guys went back to fishing. It's what they knew. It was their comfort zone.

One morning, after a particularly unproductive night of fishing, all of a sudden somebody was yelling to them from the shore: "How's the fishin'? Catch anything?"

I know from personal experience that the only time a fisherman likes to answer that question is when the icebox is full of fish. For Peter and the boys, this wasn't one of those times. They'd been out all night and hadn't caught a thing. Nothing. Nada. Zippo. Zilch. So I imagine the landlubber's question didn't go over too well.

Then the guy on the beach took it to the next level, trying to tell these professional fishermen how to do their job.

"Throw out your net on the right-hand side of the boat, and you'll get some!" (John 21:6, NLT).

"Whatever, dude." You can almost hear James or John, one of the Sons of Thunder, making a smart-aleck comment. "I'll show ya where to find some fish, buddy!"

These guys fished for a living. They knew what they were doing. Who did this yahoo think he was? I figure about now one of the more levelheaded guys, maybe Nathanael, says, "What do we have to lose? Let's give it one more toss."

"So they did, and they couldn't haul in the net because there were so many fish in it" (John 21:6, NLT).

That's all these guys needed to see. John immediately looked at Peter and said, "It's the Lord!" (John 21:7, NLT).

Before you know it, Peter is in the water doing the butterfly stroke to shore to see Jesus. You gotta love him. What follows is one of the most tender and holy moments ever recorded between two men. The love of Jesus covers the full multitude of Peter's idiotic blunders.

> When they had finished eating, Jesus said to Simon Peter, "Simon son of John, do you love me more than these?"
>
> "Yes, Lord," he said, "you know that I love you."
>
> Jesus said, "Feed my lambs."
>
> Again Jesus said, "Simon son of John, do you love me?"
>
> He answered, "Yes, Lord, you know that I love you."
>
> Jesus said, "Take care of my sheep."
>
> The third time he said to him, "Simon son of John, do you love me?"
>
> Peter was hurt because Jesus asked him the third time, "Do you love me?" He said, "Lord, you know all things; you know that I love you."
>
> Jesus said, "Feed my sheep."
>
> JOHN 21:15-17

First, notice what *didn't* happen. Jesus didn't say, "Pete, how many times are you going to mess up before you smarten up?" Jesus didn't get in his face or unload on him.

I think Jesus was probably just poking the fire with a stick, like guys do, not even looking directly at Peter. We have no way of knowing the tone of his voice, but I'm certain it was tender and kind. There was no hint of sarcasm or condemnation.

Just a simple and honest question: "Simon son of John, do you love me?"

You might be wondering, "Where do you see the love of Jesus in this exchange? Where is the love that covers a multitude of sins?" Good question. I'm glad you asked.

Look a little closer at what happened. Jesus asked the heart-penetrating question, "Do you love me?" Peter responded, "Yes, Lord." And after each verbal exchange, Jesus gave Peter a special assignment. He said, "Feed my lambs. Take care of my sheep."

The very fact that Jesus restored Peter to a position of ministry was an act of incredible love, forgiveness, and—need I say it? epic grace.

Would you put a guy like Peter in charge of anything after his biggest screwup ever? Would you entrust the care of those you just died for to a guy who abandoned you in your darkest hour? Not me. Not for a second. But Jesus did.

The grace-filled love of Jesus covered it all.

Off the Deep End

As I mentioned before, when I was twenty-two years old, I went off the deep end. I'd been married for about four years, we had two children, and I was extremely angry.

Angry at God.

Angry at myself.

Angry at everybody.

Without a doubt, the previous year had been the hardest and worst year of my life. I had left a staff position as a youth pastor at a church in Eugene to move to Spokane to help a friend of mine with his start-up church.

Candidly, it was like dropping off a cliff. I loved my job at Faith Center. I loved Eugene. God was doing an amazing thing at that church. I was growing there. It was beyond good.

Spokane? I love it now, but not then. I'll leave it at that.

Our new church, Life Center, was more like a death center for me. That first year was painful. It was horrible. The height of my ministry there was cleaning toilets and emptying trash. No glory, just guts, and not much victory, only the agony of defeat.

Let me refresh your memory with a brief list of the other things that happened that same year:

- Our firstborn daughter, Jessica, had colic and pretty much screamed constantly.
- I had the worst job of my life, selling life insurance door-to-door. It was horrible.
- We had our second child, Nathan, and he almost died.
- My folks moved to Spokane to be near us and then went through a divorce.
- My dad went through detox for the first time, but not the last.

I wish I could tell you I handled all of this with profound maturity and faith, being the spiritual giant I am. But the truth is, I got really angry.

Foolishly, I blamed God for just about everything. "If this is the way you take care of me and my family, then maybe you're not all you're cracked up to be."

As a result of all that happened, I turned inward and ugly rather than upward and holy. I let desperate times lead to desperate and foolish choices. I walked away from God.

One of the things I learned during that time is how quickly a person can become very proficient at sin. Up to that time in my life, I'd never been to a bar. I'd never been drunk. I'd never been around drugs. I didn't smoke, chew, or go with girls that do. Most of that changed overnight. I became quite the *wild thang*. Tragically, I finally found something I was good at.

I fell away and I fell hard. I wanted absolutely nothing to do with God, church, or those hypocrites called Christians. It was truly the dark ages in my life.

Guess what my dear wife did through it all? She kept loving me. She kept humbly and faithfully walking with Jesus. And the more she did, the more I disdained her. One of the great ironies of human nature is how we tend to despise the people and things that are best for us. We get so dark and broken and vile on the inside that we abhor the light in any form. We run from it like a cockroach runs when you turn on the kitchen light.

Now I was angry at Laura, too. If she wasn't going to go my way, I wasn't going to go hers. It breaks my heart to tell you this, because I remember the event all too well, but the day finally came when I told her I was through. I wanted a divorce. I was done with her, with God, with everything.

Laura is the best thing that ever happened to me. She is one of the kindest, sweetest, and most loyal people I know. If I had been her, I would have been relieved. She could have said, "Fine. Go. I can do better. I never liked the name *Bubna* anyhow!"

I deserved to have her shut me out, but she wouldn't stop loving me. And her love covered a multitude of my sins.

My wife has taught me many things, but the greatest thing I ever learned from her was unconditional love. Sure, I know God loves me. He has to. He's God. But Laura didn't have to. And yet she loved me anyway—despite my persistent idiocy.

She wouldn't let me go from her heart, no matter what I said or did. That kind of love is powerful. It's hard to resist. Why? Because it is the love of God demonstrated through flesh and blood. You can see it. You can feel it. You can touch it because it touches you.

Then she called a mutual friend, Joe Wittwer, who called another friend in the area, Steve Overman. The long and the short of it is that Laura and Steve and Joe loved me back to Jesus.

When Steve and I met at Bob's Big Boy, he had earned the right to be heard by showing me his unconditional love and acceptance over and over again. That night, Steve spoke God's words right into my heart. I was at a fork in the road with a choice between life and death. Thankfully, I chose life, and the prodigal son came home.

The fact that my wife never gave up on me amazes me to this day. Here I am, more than thirty years later, all choked up and raining tears all over my laptop. Her love for me covered everything. That's what love does—it covers a multitude of sins. She's never even once brought up any of my past failures.

The fact that God never gave up on me and has even restored me to ministry, just like he did for Peter, completely overwhelms me. I still walk with a limp, but let me tell you from firsthand experience what I know about the love and grace of God.

It's ludicrous.

It's scandalous.

It's crazy.

It's ridiculous.

It's healing and restoring.

And it always breaks my heart.

If you've wandered, or are wandering—or maybe you're running as fast as you can the other way—stop and allow God's love and grace to consume and overwhelm you. Let it cover your sins. Never forget this tremendous truth—restoration is God's specialty.

21
WHAT I DIDN'T TELL YOU

By the grace of God I am what I am,
and his grace to me was not without effect.
No, I worked harder than all of them—
yet not I, but the grace of God that was with me.

1 CORINTHIANS 15:10

I'VE USED THE WORD *IDIOT* in this book to describe myself, my actions, and the actions of others. I could tell you many more stories of lots of other stupid things I've said and done. However, though I've been stubborn, stiff-necked, and foolish way too often, the Bible teaches that those who are in relationship with Christ have a new identity and are no longer defined by their actions.

God doesn't see us the way we typically see ourselves. He doesn't see us the way others see us either. In fact, he sees us through the filter of the Cross. He sees us through the blood of his Son, Jesus. Simply put, this is the good news we call "the gospel." This is the word of hope we hold on to. We can change. Through Jesus, we can become brand-new people.

I want to make an important distinction here. Though my actions have many times been idiotic, an idiot is not who I really am.

I'm not the court jester or a royal fool.

I am a prince, a child of the King, noble and righteous in Christ.

I am special to God, and I am deeply and unconditionally loved.

Here's how Peter, a former idiot like me, puts it: "But you are a chosen people, a royal priesthood, a holy nation, God's special possession, that you may declare the praises of him who called you out of darkness into his wonderful light. Once you were not a people, but now you are the people of God; once you had not received mercy, but now you have received mercy" (1 Peter 2:9-10).

Peter states with bold word pictures that we now have a new identity. We are chosen, royal priests and holy people who now belong to God because of his grace and mercy. The images here stagger me.

I know myself, and by now you know me too. I know what I've done, yet God has set the *old* me completely out of his thoughts and view. I don't wear the dunce cap of shame any longer. I'm different now. New. Changed forever.

As I said from the beginning, it is my hope that as you have read my story you have learned some important lessons. It is my heartfelt prayer that you will learn from my blunders without having to make the same mistakes yourself. Unfortunately, we humans sometimes revert to our old ways and old identity—but we don't have to, because that is not who we really are in Christ.

The apostle Paul wrote these words to his young friend Titus:

Once we, too, were foolish and disobedient. We were misled and became slaves to many lusts and pleasures.

Our lives were full of evil and envy, and we hated each other.

But—"When God our Savior revealed his kindness and love, he saved us, not because of the righteous things we had done, but because of his mercy. He washed away our sins, giving us a new birth and new life through the Holy Spirit. He generously poured out the Spirit upon us through Jesus Christ our Savior. Because of his grace he declared us righteous and gave us confidence that we will inherit eternal life."

TITUS 3:3-7, NLT

Let these words bathe you in God's goodness: "He washed away our sins, giving us a new birth and new life. . . . Because of his grace he declared us righteous." Go ahead, read those verses again, but this time substitute *your* name for the words *our* and *us*.

God washed away Kurt's sins and gave Kurt a new birth and a new life. . . . Because of his grace he declared Kurt righteous.

Unbelievable. Incredible. Mind-blowing. Yet we find it so hard to believe sometimes and so hard to imagine that kind of change.

In my lifetime, I've experienced a whole lot of change around me:

- Phones became portable.
- Coffee became complicated and expensive.
- Mail became electronic.
- Spam became something besides canned meat.
- Music and pictures became digital.

- Cameras became disposable.
- Computers went from room-size to palm-size.
- TVs went from black and white with tubes to high definition living color on flat, plasma screens.
- Elvis is dead (at least I think so).

Change is everywhere. Change is inevitable, and change is God's plan for you and me.

Years ago, in a small church I pastored in Portland, a man showed up one Sunday who was obviously very uncomfortable. He snuck in the back just after the service started and snuck back out just before it ended. This went on for weeks. He never talked to anyone, and if I ever looked his way during my message, his eyes would immediately fall to the floor.

One day, I decided to go out a side door and track this guy down in the parking lot before he could get away. My heart broke for him because I could tell he was wounded. I just wanted him to know I was glad he was coming and that our church would be a safe place for him to discover grace.

I reached him just before he got into his car and startled him with my greeting, "Hey, thanks for coming today. What's your name?"

He started to speak, and then he grabbed his car door handle and looked as if he was going to bolt away as he mumbled, "My name is Arnie."

"Arnie, that's great!" I said. "It's really nice to meet you, man."

Without looking up he replied, "Yeah . . . it's nice to meet you, too."

And that was it.

The next Sunday, Arnie snuck in late again, but this time he waited in the back after the service long enough for me to get to him. We simply chitchatted, though I did most of the chatting, and that was the pattern we practiced for quite a while.

After a couple of months, at the end of the service one Sunday, when I invited people to experience the grace and forgiveness of God and to give their hearts and lives to Christ, Arnie came forward and began his life as a Christ-follower. I was so excited for him.

We talked after the service again that day. He was obviously moved and touched deeply by the love of God, but he asked if he could come to see me that week.

"Of course," I told him, "I'd love to sit down and hear your story." At that moment, the look on his face went from joy to terror. It wasn't until later that week that I understood why.

When Arnie and I met, he was extremely nervous. He couldn't make eye contact with me, and he sat in the chair like he was sitting on a hill of fire ants. I tried to break the ice with humor, but that didn't work. Then I reached across and put my hand on his knee and said, "Arnie, it's okay. Nothing you say can or will change my love or God's love for you in any way."

With that he started to cry and shake his head as he said, "You don't know what I've done. . . . You don't know." And then he started to weep. I pulled my chair next to his and just put my arm around him as he sobbed for a long time, saying over and over again, "You don't know . . . you don't know . . . you just don't know."

After a while, he started to tell me his story. All the things I didn't know, but that he desperately needed to tell someone. For the better part of an hour, Arnie did more talking than I'd ever heard from him before. He told me everything, sometimes in vivid detail. It was a long and sordid story of sexual sin and some pretty deviant behavior.

When he finished, for a brief moment he looked up at me eye-to-eye and man-to-man and said, "You told me that God could love anybody and forgive anything. Are you sure? Is that for real? Knowing what you know now, can you honestly tell me that God can accept and forgive a guy like me?"

Now it was my turn to cry as I had the awesome privilege of telling him, without hesitation or question, "God loves you, Arnie. He always has and always will. It is what he does. It is who he is. In fact, he delights in taking messed-up people like you and me and changing us from the inside out. Through his radical and ludicrous love-filled grace and forgiveness, we can be free."

Arnie began a journey that day that changed him forever. He began to experience the healing grace of God that set him free from his past and free from guilt and shame. He began to understand that we don't have to live trapped by our old identity.

Listen again to Paul's liberating words in Titus 3: "Once we, too, were foolish and disobedient. We were misled and became slaves to many lusts and pleasures. Our lives were full of evil. . . . But—'When God our Savior revealed his kindness and love, he saved us . . . because of his mercy. He washed away our sins.'"

Once upon a time, my primary identity was *idiot*. A fool and a slave to sin. But that is the old me. That is not who I truly am anymore.

Unfortunately, some lessons can only be learned through experience, and sometimes we insist, it seems, on learning things the hard way. I suppose some things can't be taught. They must be fleshed out to be truly understood.

But I find great comfort knowing that I am not stuck in a rut, and neither are you.

I'm not bound to my past, and neither are you.

I'm not trapped in my old identity, and neither are you.

Whatever has happened—no matter what—can be used by God to help us better become who we truly are in him. He has changed me. He *is* changing me. I am daily becoming more and more who I already am in him.

Old Guys Rule is a brand of clothes for surfers. They have a T-shirt that reads, "The older I get, the better I was." Obviously, that's not really true in my case. Yet God can and will redeem anything we give up and give over to his care. Never let that truth wander far from your soul.

I've been many things in my life, including an idiot way too often. But most of all—above all—despite what I've done and what I've been, I am God's and he is mine.

I am a chosen son, a prince, and one who belongs to the Father.

He loves me. He always has, and he always will. We don't deserve grace. We can't earn it. We can't buy it or bargain for it. All we can do is accept it and be changed by it into the image of his Son. That's the story of God's love in epic proportions!

22

IF I SHOULD WAKE
BEFORE I DIE . . .

I have come that they may have life, and have it to the full.

JOHN 10:10

PROSTATE CANCER. Two words no man ever wants to hear from his doctor. It's hard to describe the almost surreal experience when you do. You feel like a tree that has just been uprooted by a massive storm, and you're lying there in a mangled mess of broken branches.

As cancers go, if they catch this kind early enough, it's not the worst one you could have, but it's still cancer, and the potential long-term implications, such as incontinence or sexual dysfunction, are pretty scary.

For about a year or so, my doctor had been monitoring my prostate-specific antigen (PSA) levels through a simple blood test. This test is one way to see if something is going on with the prostate that shouldn't be. When my PSA levels continued to climb, the doctor recommended a biopsy.

To call this procedure invasive and embarrassing would be

a gross understatement. Think cattle prod with a needle on the end, applied in the worst possible place. The fact that it was done in the presence of a young and attractive female nurse only made it worse. I'm not sure why it mattered that she was young and attractive rather than old and ugly. But it did. It's probably pride.

Five days later—the longest five days of my life—the doctor called at 5:05 p.m. with the news. "I'm sorry to inform you that the biopsy found cancer in several of the samples taken from both sides of your prostate."

It's weird what goes through your mind when you hear something like that over the phone. For just a second I thought, *Right, good one, Doc—way to mess with my head!* Then a nanosecond later, you realize this is for real, and the doc is *not* kidding.

As you can imagine, I had a lot of questions. He said, "We need to sit down and talk so I can explain more and talk about your options."

My options? What the heck does that mean? Maybe I'll just opt out of this whole cancer thing.

"Options, like what?" I asked, wondering if I really wanted to know the answer to that question.

With almost zero emotion, he said, "Like whether you should have surgery or radiation treatments."

That's when it hit me. I really had only two options: supernatural healing or extra-natural healing. Either God was going to miraculously heal me, or I would be healed through the use of modern medicine and the gifts of a skilled physician. One way or the other, I was going to face this cancer thing until one of those two options worked or neither one did. And if they didn't succeed, I would be going home to heaven a lot sooner than I ever thought.

My wife and I did all the research we could. We spoke with several medical professionals, and I spoke with a couple of friends who've been through it.

The final decision was to try "radical prostate surgery." The doctor believed that the cancer was contained within the prostate and that it had not metastasized (i.e., spread), and so the prognosis was good.

I had a peace about the outcome. I was in God's hands before I got the news about the cancer. I was still in his hands *after* the news, and I was pretty sure God was not done with me yet.

As it turned out, the surgery was successful, and I've been cancer free for almost two years. I've also had almost no residual side effects from having my prostate removed. (How do you spell *relief*!)

Besides praying for healing, in the weeks prior to my operation, one of my most consistent prayers went like this: "God, regardless of the final outcome, what is it that you want to do in and through me throughout this ordeal?"

I hope by now you've figured out that I live with a strong conviction that life is filled with many opportunities to learn and grow along the way. What happens during our journey is meant to carve, mold, and shape us into the men and women we are meant to be. God never wastes anything. Our successes, our failures, our joys, our fears, and even our struggles with cancer can be used as a productive and holy chisel in the hands of the Great Master-Artist God.

Not for a minute did I blame God for my cancer. Not for a second did I think he *gave* this sickness to me. No human father would inflict his child with an illness just to teach him a lesson, and our heavenly Father would never do so either. The problem is, we live in a broken world with broken bodies that just get sick from time to time. Rather than wasting time and energy trying to figure out why, or who to blame, the best thing we can do is try to figure out how to cooperate with God to grow through our struggles, whatever they may be.

I'm quite certain there are many lessons I have yet to learn and a lot more God wants to do through all of this, but so much has already happened in me.

Most of my adult life I've been keenly aware of the reality of death. I know how short and precious life can be. As a pastor, I've done many funerals. I've had too many friends and family die young.

I also know that we're all dying. Even our next breath is on loan from God. Whether we live another day or a hundred more years, life on this planet is just a blip on the radar screen of eternity. I know all this. I get it.

But for most of my life, especially in my twenties and thirties, I've lived as if I'm going to remain in this body forever. My two favorite food groups were pizza and ice cream. Not good.

Over the years, I've run a lot of miles and exercised on a regular basis, but my eating habits have been horrific. I figured I could offset the junk food with a daily multivitamin, an occasional dose of bee pollen, and an extra mile or two of running after a feeding frenzy.

As I look back over my life, I realize how much time I've probably wasted on things that really don't matter in the grand scheme of things.

I've worried too much.

I've watched too much television. (There's a reason they call it the idiot box.)

I've worked too much.

Don't get me wrong. We all need to relax, and we all need some entertainment in our lives. And of course, we all need to be diligent and work hard at whatever we do. But I've never heard anyone on their deathbed say, "Wow! I wish I'd played a lot more video games in my life!"

"Too bad I didn't work more overtime when I had the chance!"

"I sure should have spent more time worrying about things I had no control over; then I'm sure my life would have been much better."

Nope. Never. What I've heard is a lot more along the lines of regret. "If only . . ."

There are truths we know in our minds, and then there are truths that get deeply marinated into our souls. We know these truths much better because we know them in our hearts.

Here is a truth that is going much deeper in me: Life is a gift; we all have a God-given purpose, so make every day count for something bigger than yourself. Live to leave a legacy.

Again, there's nothing wrong with playing hard or working hard. There's even nothing wrong with doing nothing from time to time. But at the end of the day, and more important, at the end of your life, did you leave your handprint on this world?

Did you make a difference in the lives of those around you?

Did you live deliberately and on purpose?

Did you aspire to reach some God-given goals that changed you and others around you?

Did you live in a deep awareness of God's epic grace and goodness in your life? And did you extend that unmerited kindness to others more often than not?

I know it's somewhat morbid and perhaps a bit melodramatic to think about, but what are your family and friends going to say about you at your funeral? What will they share in your eulogy?

As children, we're taught to pray in our nighttime routine, "If I should die before I wake, I pray the Lord my soul to take." But is that it? "God, if I kick the bucket tonight, I hope I make it!"

God help us—no! His plan for us is so much better.

My prayer of late is more like this: "Father, I pray that I will wake before I die. Wake me from any lethargy. Wake me from any monotony. Wake me from a life of mediocrity. Wake me from the lie that there's nothing I can significantly contribute to this life or to the lives of others. Wake me up to what really matters."

Life really is a gift; what we do with it is up to us.

One of my favorite lines from one of my most favorite movies, *Braveheart*, goes like this: "Every man dies; not every man really lives." How incredibly true.

The single greatest certainty in life is that death comes to us all. One of the greatest uncertainties is whether we will fully live the way we were meant to live.

Life is meant to be epic! As epic as the grace of God in your life is his desire for you to live a life of adventure. His plan for you is an overflowing life lived to the max. We were made for so much more. Whatever time you and I have left, let's live it with purpose and with gusto.

It's not about how famous you are; it is about how *faithful* you are. Whether you're a single mom, a grade-school teacher, a salesman, a postman, a pastor, a doctor, a politician, or Bono from U2, use the gifts God has given you right where you are. Discover and faithfully use all the available resources of heaven to make a difference in your world, in your sphere of influence. You are God's work of art, and he has something profound planned for you.

Find it.

Go for it.

Live it, and live it gracefully.

Whether I have a few weeks, a few years, or a few decades left in this old earth suit remains to be seen. But here's what I know for certain: No matter what comes my way, no matter what I know or don't know about my future—I know the one who knows all things, and it is well with my soul.

Whatever else happens, I'm going to live to make every moment count for something bigger and greater than myself. I'm going to pursue something eternal and something reflective of God's astounding and epic grace!

So here's my prayer for you:

May you know the splendor of God's grace, the depth of his love, and the magnificence of his kindness more and more in your life . . . for it truly is epic.

May you experience God's favor and blessing in a way that continually surprises and delights you as you discover and walk in your God-given purpose.

May you always remember that, despite your obvious failings, God is drawn to you (you're a grace magnet) and will never fail or forsake you.

And may you shine as a trophy of his grace in declaration to a watching world that God is good . . . all the time.

Amen—make it so, Lord Jesus!

ACKNOWLEDGMENTS

I NEED TO GIVE SPECIAL RECOGNITION to those who made
this book possible:

My twin-from-another-mother, the amazing author
Ronna Snyder. Your insights and advice were priceless!
I could not have written this book without your help,
encouragement, and wisdom.

My daughter, Jessica Harris—thanks for the many times
you have proofed your daddy's stuff.

My friends Sally Stratton, Lindsay Noll, and Dara
Murphy—thanks for your early editing help.

My agent, Esther Fedorkevich with Fedd and Company,
and my publisher, Jan Long Harris and her amazing
staff at Tyndale Momentum. It truly does take a team
to produce anything of value. Special thanks to Dave
Lindstedt, an extraordinary editor, who made me a
better me.

And of course, my dear and amazing wife, Laura. She's
read this thing about a dozen times and keeps me
honest and accurate. Did I mention yet how much
I love you, honey?

No life is lived or work completed without the love, help, and
support of friends and family. I thank God for each of you. You
have been used by God to help mold me and shape me into the
man that I am.

As iron sharpens iron, so a friend sharpens a friend.

PROVERBS 27:17, NLT

NOTES

1. Brennan Manning, *Reflections for Ragamuffins* (New York: HarperCollins, 1998), 157. Manning attributes the quote to his spiritual director, Larry Hein.
2. Living Water International, http://www.water.cc.
3. Compassion International, http://www.compassion.com/poverty/water.htm.
4. Jerry Cook with Stanley C. Baldwin, *Love, Acceptance and Forgiveness*, second edition (Ventura, CA: Regal, 2009), 12.
5. *The Autobiography of Martin Luther King Jr.*, edited by Clayborne Carson (New York: Warner Books, 1998), 61.

DISCUSSION GUIDE

THIS GUIDE IS DESIGNED for a four-week individual or group study of *Epic Grace*. Within each week, the questions are broken out by chapter so you can adjust for a shorter or longer study, if needed. Feel free to focus on the questions or issues that resonate the most with you; the guide is intended to be a starting point for deeper community and personal spiritual growth, so use it as a base and let God guide your time.

In each week's section, you'll find one or more QR codes leading to a special video with Kurt. He shares "gracelets"—personal stories from people who've discovered God's epic grace in their own experiences—and invites you to go deeper into the message of *Epic Grace*. Snap the code with your smartphone or visit the link below each code to access the video.

Week 1: Read the introduction and chapters 1–5

Start your *Epic Grace* journey here with a message from Kurt.

www.tyndal.es/
epicgrace1

Introduction: First of All . . .

1. Kurt says that when he started writing this book, he knew two words had to be in the title: *grace* and *idiot*. What words would be important to include in the story of your own life?
2. Do you ever share Kurt's feeling of being overwhelmed or inadequate, or wonder why God would choose to use you? What experiences tend to bring on these feelings?
3. When you hear the words *epic grace*, what first comes to mind? What aspect of this phrase intrigues you? What do you hope to learn about epic grace by reading this book?

www.tyndal.es/
epicgrace2

Chapter 1: The Last Two Miles

1. Kurt says that "life's most valuable and lasting lessons are often learned in the dark valleys of defeat and despair." Has this been your experience? What are some of the lessons you've learned?
2. The stories of Job, Kurt's grandson, and Margaret are three examples of *overcoming* that Kurt shares in this chapter. What are some examples of victory over suffering that inspire you from the Bible, from history, or from your own life?

3. Kurt says that although his family trusted God and survived the tragedy of losing Phineas, "it took a while for me to come to the place where I could fall on my face and worship." Can you relate to this during hard times? How do you think God responds to us in those moments?

www.tyndal.es/
epicgrace3

4. Kurt shares some of the questions he wrestles with, including, *Why did my grandson die?* and *Why didn't God answer my prayer the way I wanted it answered?* What does Kurt hold on to in the face of not knowing the answers? How would you respond to a friend going through a similar situation who had these questions?

Chapter 2: Driven by Destiny

1. Do you agree with Kurt that we all need to find our God-given niche? Would you say you've found yours? If so, what is it? If not, what dreams might you pursue?

2. Kurt says too many people have gone into professional ministry because it seemed the only legitimate way to serve God. Do you agree with this? How might people live out discovering and sharing God's epic grace through other career paths?

3. Read these passages that talk about living the life God has called us to: Genesis 12:1-4; Luke 9:21-26; Ephesians 2:1-10. What do they tell you about your destiny in God?

Chapter 3: Prone to Wander

1. Looking back on the time he left vocational ministry, claiming that God had "released" him, Kurt ponders, "Why do we Christians tend to spiritualize our own stupidity?" How would you answer this question?

2. Have you ever had a friend like Steve Overman—someone who walked with you through the dark times and encouraged you to stay true to God and yourself? What was it about that person (something he or she did, was, or said) that got through to you?

3. In what areas in your life has it been difficult for you to stay the course? How has this affected your life? How has this affected the lives of your family and/or friends?

Chapter 4: God's Algebra

1. In describing his dysfunctional childhood, Kurt says it taught him two things: "My value to God and others is based solely on my performance" and "My worth is measured by my success." What "lessons" did you learn from your own childhood (whether it was a healthy one or not) that you later discovered weren't really true?

2. Kurt says that even though he feared and avoided his dad, he still wanted to please him. How do you think growing up like this might affect a person's understanding of God as our Father?

3. Coming to understand God's unconditional love has been vital to Kurt's faith journey. As you consider the attributes of God, which ones have special significance to you?

4. What did finding something as small as a shell ultimately teach Kurt about epic grace?

Chapter 5: The Curse of Comparison

1. What are some of the things you have caught yourself measuring against others in your life: brains, beauty, money, success, power?

2. Kurt shares the story of the basketball coach who was discouraging and dismissive. Do you have a story of a teacher, counselor, or role model who either dismissed your gifts in a hurtful way or called out your talents in a positive way? How has that experience shaped you? What has it taught you about grace or judgment?

3. Read these passages that talk about comparison: 1 Corinthians 12:4-6; 2 Corinthians 12:9; Romans 15:7. What do these passages tell you about the value of our uniqueness in Christ?

Week 2: Read chapters 6–10

Chapter 6: All for a Roll in the Hay?

1. Kurt says of his early indiscretions: "I repented over and over. In fact, I must have 'gotten saved' a dozen times during that season of my life." Yet he continued to make the same mistakes. Why do you think it can be so hard to turn your back on sin?

2. Consider the story of Jacob and Esau. Have you ever sold out for something less than you were worth because it seemed quicker and more satisfying at the moment?

3. What might have been different for Kurt's friend Hank if he had called someone for help? What might have happened if that person had shared with him God's message of epic grace?

Chapter 7: Modern-Day Pharisees

1. What are the two principles that Kurt says he practices (see page 68)? How do they compare to the core principles you live by?

2. Do you agree with Kurt that Jesus would have joined the neighborhood block party? Why or why not?

3. Kurt says that what others think of us is not as important as what God thinks about us. How do you reconcile this with the biblical encouragement to hold one another accountable and seek godly counsel? What is the difference between acting out of fear for your reputation and making wise decisions?

Chapter 8: "Mommy, Why Does He Walk Funny?"

1. Why does Kurt believe that people who limp are also grace-driven people? Has this been your own experience, or have you encountered people whose limps have made them bitter? What do you think makes the difference?

2. Read these passages that talk about God's redeeming the past: John 21:1-23; Romans 8:28-30; Ephesians 2:1-10; Revelation 3:14-22. What, if anything, is required of us for God to redeem the past? What do these passages tell you about who God is?

www.tyndal.es/
epicgrace4

Chapter 9: You Don't Want to Read about This

1. In this chapter, Kurt shares a personal story that he hesitated to make public. What were some of his fears in doing so? Why does he say he finally decided to share this experience?

2. Has someone in your life ever decided to take a risk in sharing a story or a secret with you? How did you respond? How did it affect your relationship?

3. How does Kurt say our understanding of epic grace should shape our attitude toward those who have hurt us?

Chapter 10: This Little Piggy Went to Market

1. How might Kurt's reflection that "providing for my every need is God's job; managing with wisdom what I have is mine" affect your financial choices, particularly in difficult economic times?

2. Do you need to be more faithful with any of the gifts (or talents) God has given you?

3. Can you share a story or experience about a financial lesson you learned the hard way?

4. Considering your current financial situation, what do you think God is trying to teach you about himself? About yourself? About life?

Week 3: Read chapters 11–16

Chapter 11: Learning to Love a VDP

1. Has there been anyone in your life that you've struggled to love? How has this person affected your life? How has your learning to love "the least of these" affected the lives of your family and/or friends?

2. Kurt compares the membership of the Tujunga church to King David's "band of misfits." What role do you see "misfits" playing throughout Scripture? Why do you think outcasts seem at times to be especially close to the heart of God?

Chapter 12: What Those Romance Novels Don't Tell You

1. Do you share Kurt's experience of falling into the belief that we are somehow promised comfort and happiness in this life, and then feeling blindsided when trouble comes (even though Jesus guaranteed it would)? Where do you think this expectation comes from?

2. Can you think of an experience in your own life when you stuck it out through the valleys and ended up with joy you wouldn't have encountered if you'd given up during the hardest time?

Chapter 13: Lost!

1. What spiritual parallels can you draw in your own life from Kurt's rules of mountain climbing: (1) have the right gear and (2) never climb alone; stay with your group?

2. What do you think of the sentiment: "I don't need the church. I've got Jesus, and that's good enough"?

3. Why do you think some people tend to isolate and insulate rather than take full advantage of the community of faith we have in Christ?

Chapter 14: Wild Hogs

1. Do you agree with Kurt that God never meant for us to be alone? Can you think of any biblical examples of people seeking solitude (in a positive or negative way)? How can you tell the difference between when you genuinely need one-on-one time with God and when you are isolating yourself or hiding?

2. Kurt mentions the movie *Wild Hogs* as one that reflects a true and sustaining friendship. What are some other movies or books that demonstrate the principles of good friendship to you?

Chapter 15: Lessons I Learned on a Scooter

1. Kurt says, "God will use whatever means necessary to create in us the likeness and character of his Son"— including an embarrassing mode of transportation. Has there been a "scooter" in your own life—something humbling that you didn't want, but that God used to develop your character?
2. Have you experienced a test of the *unknown, unfulfilled,* or *unforeseen*? How did you respond to it? How was your experience similar to, or different from, that of Abraham?

Chapter 16: Caleb

1. What has loving Caleb taught Kurt about our adoption into the family of God? Why do you think this is a particularly poignant message for someone with Kurt's childhood experiences?
2. Kurt says, "Nothing . . . rips my heart to shreds faster than to see my children suffer. I would give anything to spare my kids the pain they have gone through." What has parenthood taught him about the love of God the Father? Have you ever wished you could take someone else's pain on yourself to spare them? What has this taught you about the Cross?

3. Do you resonate with the heart-cry in this chapter: "I *know* I need to trust. I *know* God's grace is sufficient. I just wish I could see what's going on"? How does it affect you to know that there may be a Caleb waiting for you on the other side of your pain, even though you can't see it yet?

www.tyndal.es/
epicgrace5

Week 4: Read chapters 17–22

Chapter 17: Dreams and Darkness and Demons! Oh My!

1. Has there ever been a time when God powerfully grabbed your attention through a dream?

2. Do you agree with Kurt about the reasons God might give you a dream, vision, or picture of something? How do you think you might tell the difference between a dream that comes from God and one that doesn't?

3. As you think through your own family history, can you see a common dark struggle? What have you or others done by God's grace to break negative generational cycles?

Chapter 18: Bushwhacked!

1. Every family has at least one horror story. Share your story of a family trip or day that was supposed to be epic but turned into a disaster of epic proportions!

2. Kurt was committed to his plan for the day, even when it wasn't working out. How do you decide whether it's wisest to "stay the course" or come up with a new plan?

3. Do you agree with Kurt that blame and shame *never* produce anything good in anyone? What would you say is the difference between shame and healthy regret with repentance?

www.tyndal.es/
epicgrace6

Chapter 19: The Problem with Expectations

1. Think about the last time you had a conflict with someone. How did unmet expectations play a role in that conflict?
2. Can you spot any patterns in your own life that might be the result of unmet (or even unrealistic) expectations?
3. What do you cling to when you feel as if God has let you down?

Chapter 20: What's Love Got to Do with It?

1. Why does Kurt say he relates to the apostle Peter so much? Which biblical character do you find you relate to the most?
2. Do you agree with Kurt that "one of the great ironies of human nature is how we tend to despise the people and things that are best for us"? Why or why not?
3. How does Kurt describe his wife's love for him, and what did it show him about God? If you had a friend in Laura's situation, what advice might you give her? Would your advice be different if the outcome of Kurt and Laura's story wasn't a happy one?

Chapter 21: What I Didn't Tell You

1. What does Kurt reveal in this chapter about why he's okay with describing himself as an idiot? Do you feel confident in your own true identity?

2. Can you relate to the questions Arnie asks of Kurt in this chapter? What do you think about Kurt's answer?

3. What have you learned in this chapter and in the book overall about what makes God's grace epic?

Chapter 22: If I Should Wake Before I Die . . .

1. Kurt says, "As I look back over my life, I realize how much time I've probably wasted on things that really don't matter in the grand scheme of things." At the end of your life, what will be the things you've done "too much"? What might you do today to replace one of them with something you're currently doing "not enough"?

2. What does Kurt's desire to "wake before I die" mean to you? From what do you need to awaken?

3. What is something epic you still want to happen in your life or faith? Pray to God that it will be accomplished through his grace.

www.tyndal.es/
epicgrace7

ABOUT THE AUTHOR

KURT BUBNA has been in pastoral ministry since 1976 and now serves as the lead pastor of Eastpoint Church, a large, growing, creative, and community-focused congregation in Spokane Valley, Washington (www.eastpointchurch.org). He passionately believes that the church should be a safe place to discover grace.

Bivocational during much of his twenties, Kurt was very successful in the banking industry for almost ten years. He has also traveled extensively as a speaker, worship leader, and short-term missionary in Great Britain, Mexico, Guatemala, Nepal, India, and Sri Lanka. For more information about his speaking availability and engagements, please see www.KurtBubna.com.

His hobbies include playing multiple instruments, long walks with his wife of more than thirty-eight years, and even longer rides on his motorcycle (the best midlife crisis therapy in the world). He also loves to jump out of perfectly good airplanes, and anything and everything to do with the deep blue sea!

Kurt is a son, brother, husband, father of four plus their four spouses, uncle of many, grandfather of the tribe, and pastor of an amazing group of fellow sojourners. But most of all, he is a child of God and humbled by God's epic grace.

Online Discussion *guide*

TAKE *your* TYNDALE READING EXPERIENCE *to the* NEXT LEVEL

A FREE discussion guide for this book is available at bookclubhub.net, perfect for sparking conversations in your book group or for digging deeper into the text on your own.

www.bookclubhub.net

You'll also find free discussion guides for other Tyndale books, e-newsletters, e-mail devotionals, virtual book tours, and more!

"THINK MONTY PYTHON MEETS C. S. LEWIS."
—*Relevant Magazine*

Matt Mikalatos liked Jesus a lot. In fact, he couldn't believe how much they had in common. They shared the same likes, dislikes, beliefs, and opinions (though Jesus did have better hair). So imagine Matt's astonishment when he finds out that the guy he knows as Jesus . . . *isn't*. He's an Imaginary Jesus: a comfortable, convenient imitation Matt has created in his own image. The real Jesus is still out there somewhere . . . and Matt is determined to find him.

A fast-paced, sort-of-true story, *My Imaginary Jesus* is a wild spiritual adventure like nothing you've ever read before . . . and It might bring you face-to-face with an impostor in your own life.

ISBN 978-1-4143-6473-5